CHRISTIANITY AND HUMAN
RELATIONS IN INDUSTRY

The Beckly Social Service Lecture

Frank Myers,
Bellshill.
January 23rd 1952.

CHRISTIANITY AND HUMAN RELATIONS IN INDUSTRY

by

SIR GEORGE SCHUSTER
K.C.S.I., K.C.M.G., C.B.E., M.C.

LONDON : THE EPWORTH PRESS

PUBLISHED BY

THE EPWORTH PRESS
(FRANK H. CUMBERS)
25–35 CITY ROAD, LONDON, E.C.1

*

New York . Toronto
Melbourne . Capetown

*

SET IN MONOTYPE BASKERVILLE AND PRINTED BY
THE CAMELOT PRESS LTD., LONDON AND SOUTHAMPTON

CONTENTS

ONE

INTRODUCTORY

I HAVE chosen as my subject 'Christianity and Human Relations in Industry'. My conception of 'industry' is not one of a mechanical process concerned with material production, but of a vast complex of human activities and human relations. This conception is an essential foundation for a true appreciation of what a Christian attitude in industry means; but it is also essential for a right approach to the practical problem of getting the best results in terms of production. It is indeed a curious paradox that the mechanization of industry actually increases the importance of the human problem, since the adjustment of men to highly mechanized work by its very nature and scale requires a high degree of co-operation. The experience of the last war brought this out. Never has warfare been so highly mechanized and yet never has it been so necessary to pay attention to human considerations. But this, of course, will not be my main theme. I shall be concerned primarily, not with production results, but with the ways in which industrial work affects the lives of the men and women engaged in it.

I must give a further explanation of my title. In speaking of 'industry' I shall be thinking chiefly of employment in manufacturing industry; but the same principles hold good for employment in every form of economic enterprise where numbers of people are working together in an organized activity.

Finally, in order to make clear the scope of my subject, I must add this: I shall be concerned essentially with the behaviour of people *within* the sphere of industrial work;

but no situation in a factory can be fully understood without a knowledge of the external social setting. That must be appreciated, although I shall not be able to deal fully with all that it means.

There are some other questions which I must consider in this introductory passage.

The Founder's Purpose

Whoever is honoured by an invitation to give one of these lectures must ask himself whether he is in agreement with the Founder's purpose, which was 'to set forth the social implications of Christianity and to further the development of a Christian sociology, and the experience of the Christian attitude in reference to social, industrial, economic, and international subjects'. It is important to bear these exact words in mind. I think they are well phrased, and I accept the purpose with my whole heart. I believe profoundly that Christians and the Christian Churches should concern themselves with studying how Christian principles can be applied to the handling of worldly problems. Otherwise there can be no meaning in praying, as we do every day, that the Kingdom of God may come and the Will of God may be done, in earth as it is in Heaven. I agree, too, with Dr. Scott Lidgett's exposition in the Introduction to his 1938 lecture, from which I will select two quotations:

Heaven is the sphere of absolute values that are realized and active in the living God and are participated in by those who are in fellowship with Him as His sons. *Yet these values are implanted in true human life, are organic with it, and can only be pursued in so far as they gain practical expression in character and social conduct* (p. 20).[1]

And again:

The influence of Christ's spirit enables His followers to seize opportunities, to overcome obstacles, and to utilize all avail-

[1] The italics are mine.

able instruments to give effect to the dictates of the love of God 'shed abroad' in their hearts and activating them to sacrificial effort *for the redemption and fulfilment of human nature, in the light of the eternal values and of their temporal demands*.[2]

And to these I might add some words written by Florence Nightingale:

We can only act and speak and think through God; and what we need is to discover such laws of His as will enable us to be always thinking in conscious concert with Him. There will be no Heaven unless we make it, and it is a very poor Theodike which teaches us that we are not to 'prepare' for this world, but only to 'prepare' for another. Must we not 'possess' God here if we are to possess Him hereafter? Desire for personal salvation is not religion.[3]

There is of course much more to be said on this subject; I need do no more at this stage than make my position broadly clear. My interpretation of that position will reveal itself more fully as I follow out my discussion of the way in which Christians should concern themselves with the particular group of worldly problems which I have chosen for my theme.

The Distinctive Problems of the Present Time

I turn from this to another introductory reflection.

Each of these lectures is one of a continuous series which, it must be hoped, will extend year by year over a long period. Each lecturer should, as I see it, take account of the conditions and problems which chiefly characterize the time when he is speaking. He should ask himself: 'In what form is the Christian message chiefly needed today? What are the problems which above all demand attention?' What he says should therefore in a sense be topical; but running through the whole series, as a continuous thread, there should be an appreciation of the eternal

[2] The italics are mine.
[3] *Florence Nightingale*, by Cecil Woodham Smith, p. 525 (Constable).

and unchanging truths of Christ's teaching. The very variation in the nature of the problems to be solved, or dangers to be countered, should help to make clear the essential significance of the eternal and unchanging truths.

In thinking of what are the distinctive characteristics of the present time, certain things stand out. First, this is a period of great uncertainty. Man has developed scientific powers capable of wrecking the whole worldly civilization, and, indeed, as I write these words in December 1950 I cannot avoid the thought that, by the date fixed for your Conference in 1951, we may be involved in a catastrophe which will make all conferences impossible. Secondly, this is a period of revolutionary change: everywhere old traditions have been broken and men are seeking to build anew in various ways and to find a new foundation for faith. Thirdly, it is a period when we have just seen—and, alas! can still see—evidence all around us of the unfathomable depths of evil to which human beings can sink, if they work in the belief that they themselves can determine their conduct without regard for any higher law. These characteristics have a significant importance for us, partly because they confirm and illuminate the eternal truths of Christ's teaching, and partly because they give to those who are alive today and who can influence the handling of human affairs (and we can all do something) a unique responsibility and opportunity.

I want to turn next to a more subtle change which seems to have come about during the course of the years since 1926 (when this lecture series was started)—a change in emphasis on the various aspects of our problems which seems to me to be brought out by considering some of the earlier lectures. I will take two of these to illustrate my point.

Sir Josiah Stamp, in the first lecture in 1926, looked at

that field of human activities which I have taken as the chief subject for my own lecture—the field of economic enterprise. He discussed a widely ranging variety of aspects, but, throughout, his main attention seems to me to have been concentrated on the external results of economic enterprise, and on examining such questions as whether its proceeds were fairly divided and what would happen if Christian principles regulated the methods of division.

How the proceeds are divided is, indeed, an important question—and I shall have something to say about it later—but it does not seem to me to be the question which matters most when one is considering the application of Christian principles to the conduct of industry. That I see rather as the question of how men should behave to each other *within* the complex network of human relations involved. I believe that the conditions of today bring this out much more clearly than was apparent in 1926.

I turn next to Dr. Scott Lidgett's lecture, given in 1938. I have already expressed my profound agreement with his general conceptions; but there is one phrase in his opening remarks which illustrates the point which I now want to make. He interprets 'the object of the generous founder of the Beckly Trust as being that of bringing the convinced support of the Christian Church, and of Methodism in particular, to aid the cause of constructive social reform in all its manifold concerns'. A few lines later he uses the phrase 'social reconstruction'. It is on these phrases 'social reform' and 'social reconstruction' that I wish to comment. I would not for a moment deny that measures of 'social reform', in the sense of changes in external forms regulating the shape of society and the conduct of human activities, have been desperately needed and that there is still a vast amount to be done. Nor do I for a moment question that actual measures, like the Education Act of 1944, the National Health Scheme, and all the wide range of social security measures which have recently been developed can be of lasting value and help to promote social progress in the truest sense. But what I do want to emphasize, and what I think current happenings bring out most clearly, is that external measures alone are not enough, and that they can indeed lead to positive evils, unless the men and women who administer them, or who take advantage of them, are guided by the right spirit both in their own actions and in their relations with their fellow men. And I want to urge that this, above all, is the message that is needed today, just because so much has been done recently in the way of external measures and because in today's political campaigns the whole emphasis appears to be on material conditions.

The Need for a Clear Statement of Christian Principles

I want to mention one other introductory reflection. Looking over the past series, it seems fair to say that the lecturers fall broadly into two classes. They have been either, on the one hand, theologians who, starting from their reflections on Christian principles, have gone forward to consider the application of these principles to some particular aspect of worldly activities, or, on the other hand, men whose lives have been concerned with the practical conduct of worldly affairs and who have examined the problems thrown up by their experience and sought to bring these problems back to Christ's teaching for guidance. The distinction has some significance; but I do not wish to exaggerate it. If the purpose of these lectures is to be fulfilled each class must take account of both sides. The 'theologians' must have an accurate appreciation of worldly problems; the 'practical men' must truly interpret Christian principles. I can only regard myself as belonging to the latter class, and, in view of what I have said, I feel bound to start with a statement of my own interpretation of Christian principles.[4] I do so with great diffidence, comparing my qualifications with some of the earlier speakers and knowing that my statement must be a very simple one—almost naïvely so.

This leads me to a digression which I hope you will excuse. I venture to urge (and this, indeed, is another reflection prompted by my reading of the special conditions of these times) that the paramount need today is for a simple message on 'wavelengths' to which ordinary people with their modern forms of thought can 'tune in'. 'Simple,' of course, does not mean superficial. To distil a simple message, to be ready with simple answers which are yet fundamentally true and thus universally applicable, requires deep thought. But deep thought, if it leads to complex expression, fails to make its contribution to mankind. I do not claim that my own simple statement meets this need. Rather I am voicing a plea as one who himself wants help. In stating this plea, I have in mind St. Paul's words:[5]

So likewise ye, except ye utter by the tongue words easy to be understood, how shall it be known what is spoken? for ye shall speak into the air.... In the Church I had rather speak five words with my understanding, that by my voice I might teach others also, than ten thousand words in an unknown tongue.

The Essential Christian Principles for Application in Industry

But this, as I have said, is a digression, and I must now turn to my own elementary statement of the essential

[4] I feel the more impelled to do this because Stamp in parts of his lecture implied an interpretation which I think is misleading. He makes a great deal of what he calls 'the Palestinian precept' of 'going two miles whenever there existed an obligation to go one mile' (p. 13), and has devoted a section (p. 57) to considering 'A society framed on the extra mile principle' and he talks of 'divergence from the economic' being prescribed. I think there is a confusion of ideas in this. Then, again, he seems to imply at many points that the case for the application of Christian principles must rest on its being possible to prove 'the power of the ethical factor to improve the standard of life'. That in my view is a totally wrong approach. I happen to believe that observance of Christian principles would improve production results, but that is not the reason for observing them.

[5] 1 Corinthians 14⁹⁻¹⁹.

Christian principles which have to be interpreted and applied in that sphere of worldly activity which I am to discuss. My belief is that everything that matters can be found in Christ's answer to the question: Which is the great commandment in the law? 'Thou shalt love the Lord thy God with all thy heart, and with all thy soul, and with all thy mind. This is the first and great commandment. And the second is like unto it, Thou shalt love thy neighbour as thyself.'[6]

If men's conduct is governed by love of their neighbours properly interpreted, if their actions are based on the belief that God has a purpose in the world with which their work must be harmonized, and if their work is seen as something dedicated to an ever-present God, then there need be no problems in human relations in any field of worldly life.

The two commandments must, of course, be considered together. Unless men respect the first there can be no sure foundation for their fulfilment of the second. I see this as one of the fundamental truths which human history—and especially recent history—makes clear. But it is the second commandment which gives us the chief guidance in relation to the purpose of these Beckly Lectures, and it is the second which above all contains the distinctive essence of Christianity, and of the new revelation of God's purpose which was given by Christ's life and teaching.

Reflections on Christ's Two Commandments

Now, as this brings us to the heart of the matter, I want to record one reflection which has always impressed me. It is a reflection which has doubtless been expressed many times before, and may be very familiar to you. If so, you must forgive me. I am simply trying to give an account of how my own thinking has worked out.

It has always seemed to me that the essential signific-

[6] Matthew 22$^{37-9}$.

ance of Christ's message can be understood still more clearly if one realizes that His two commandments were quotations from the Old Testament[7] and if one looks back to the setting from which each was taken.

Take the setting of the first in Deuteronomy. The commandment is followed by this passage:

And these words, which I command thee this day, *shall be in thine heart*: and thou shalt teach them diligently unto thy children, and shalt talk of them when thou sittest in thine house, and when thou walkest by the way, and when thou liest

---

[7] There is a point here which has puzzled and interested me. The words of the first commandment as given in Matthew 22 are not exactly identical with those in Deuteronomy. The latter says: 'Thou shalt love the Lord thy God with all thine heart, and with all thy soul, and with all thy *might*.' The words in Matthew 22 are: 'Thou shalt love the Lord thy God with all thy heart, and with all thy soul, and with all thy *mind*.' In the other two Gospel passages (Mark 12[30] and Luke 10[27]) where Christ endorses these two commandments, the words 'with all thy mind' are also used, though in these two passages the words 'with all thy strength' are added, so that in these cases the expression 'with all thy mind' is additional to, and not in substitution for, the expression 'with all thy might' in Deuteronomy. For me the words 'with all thy mind' have always had a special significance, and it is a significance to which I attach considerable weight in later passages of this lecture. That significance would be greatly increased if one could think that Christ, in taking up the words of the Old Testament, had deliberately made this addition. A most eminent theologian, with whom I have discussed the matter, writes to me as follows:

'The position is not quite clear, but it is quite certain that "with all thy *mind*" in Matthew 22[37] is not meant as a substitute for "with all thy might" in Deuteronomy 6[5]. For one thing, the Deuteronomic phrase "with all thy might" is used by Christ as recorded in Mark 12[30], "with all thy strength", and used by the lawyer, approved by Christ, in Luke 10[27]. And in this last Lucan passage, the words "with all thy mind" appear as apparently part of the *schema* repeated twice a day by the pious Jew of our Lord's day. But there is no equivalent of it in our version of the Old Testament. The Greek for this phrase here is *dianoia* (thought), with the force of "intention" and "purpose". None of the ancient peoples separated the thinking part of man so sharply from the desires, intentions, and will as we moderns do. Then I find that the phrase "with all thy might" has usually an adverbial sense, meaning "with force" or "exceedingly". On the whole the words "heart", "soul", "strength", and "mind", are fairly synonymous and their addition is a cumulative expression to mean "whole-heartedly", with no reservations. I don't think therefore Christ changed anything; there must have been a clause "with all thy mind" somewhere in the Jewish law—and though He leaves out "strength" in one place He uses it in another.'

In the light of this explanation, it would not be justifiable to attach great significance to the *difference* between the Old Testament words and the words recorded in the Gospel, but the significance of the words themselves remains as great as ever.

down, and when thou risest up. And thou shalt bind them for a sign upon thine hand, and they shall be as frontlets between thine eyes. And thou shalt write them upon the posts of thy house and on thy gates (Deuteronomy 6⁶⁻⁹).

Thus the first commandment stands out in the Old Testament with an emphasis which no language could make more impressive. But it is a very different matter when one turns to the second. The words 'Thou shalt love thy neighbour as thyself' (Leviticus 19¹⁸) are taken out of a list of many precepts covering the breeding of cattle, the use of good seed for sowing, the kindly act of leaving some grain in the fields or some grapes in the vineyards ungathered so that the poor may find something to glean from them. But Christ took, to stand by themselves, just those seven words, 'Thou shalt love thy neighbour as thyself', and by doing this, and by His own life, instilled them with a completely new significance.

The Central Question is the Interpretation of Christ's Second Commandment

All these thoughts have thus brought me to the simple statement that what I chiefly have to consider is how the words 'Thou shalt love thy neighbour as thyself' are to be interpreted and applied in the conduct of industrial enterprise, and particularly in the handling of the complex problems of human relations which are involved in our modern industrial organization.

Some Definitions

To begin with, I must make clear what I am talking about. What does the phrase 'human relations' cover? In answering this question, I shall have to make use of the common terms 'management'⁸ and 'workers' with their

---

⁸ I shall not make any attempt in my general discussion to draw the distinction between 'management' and 'owners' or employers. It will be necessary to take account of this in the section dealing with the economic

implication of 'two sides' in industry. I do not like these terms. All equally should be 'workers', and our whole purpose should be to move away from the conception of *two sides* (whose interests are in conflict) and toward the conception of a single community working with a common purpose. But, even if one takes this view, one must recognize that there is a real distinction between two kinds of groups and two kinds of responsibilities, which would remain valid even if a perfect spirit of co-operation could be developed.

The Three Aspects of Human Relations in Industry

I must therefore use these expressions and, using them, I can explain what is involved best by saying that there are three aspects or elements to be considered in human relations in industry: first, the behaviour of 'management' to 'workers'; secondly, the response of the workers (their attitude to management and to their work); and, thirdly, the relations of the workers[9] with each other (the association and co-operation of the individual with his fellow workers, which includes the important matter of relations with trade unions). Here again, while recognizing a distinction between these three elements, I do not want to overstress it. It is a help to clear thinking, but all the time one must realize that in practice no single one of the three elements can exist in isolation, and that there can be no satisfactory co-operation unless all the three kinds of relation work together in harmony.

system; but for my general discussion of the relations between the 'two sides' the distinction does not essentially matter. Incidentally, I think James Burnham, in his *Managerial Revolution*, has made too much of it.

[9] This includes all who are working in industry in whatever grade and not merely manual workers. Thus for example, the relations of the works manager with the sales manager are covered by this phrase.

TWO

THE FIRST ASPECT OF HUMAN RELATIONS IN INDUSTRY—THE RELATIONS OF MANAGEMENT WITH WORKERS

Now I PROPOSE to examine my subject in the first place by following out what I have called the 'management-worker' aspect of human relations, with emphasis on the role and responsibility of the former. That is the right emphasis, since, as things are today, the initiating responsibility rests on management. But it is essential throughout to remember that this is not the only aspect and that the other two are involved in every situation.

Some General Ideas

(i) *Mere goodwill is not enough*. Taking this line I start with some general ideas.

The first of these is that mere goodwill is not enough. To find ways for giving effect to Christ's second commandment in the conditions of modern industry is a hard problem. It cannot be solved without patient study and full understanding. It demands the best intellectual effort of which men are capable. And here I turn back once more to Christ's words. The first commandment enjoins the love of God, not only 'with all thy heart, and with all thy soul', but also 'with all thy *mind*'. When Christ said 'the second is like unto it' I think He meant that these last words applied to that commandment equally with the first. He meant that we must devote all our intellectual ability (all our 'talents') to finding practicable ways and means for fulfilling the love of our neighbour in daily life. And this effort with the *mind* is required not only in working out the best practicable arrangements for the direct handling of human relations in industry. It has another and even more important aspect. The primary duty of those who carry managerial responsibilities is to be efficient at their tasks. This must be regarded as an ethical obligation. The chances of success in creating the material foundations for a satisfactory industrial democracy and in providing good lives for the workers in it depend on the functional efficiency of management. No amount of kind-heartedness will compensate for functional inefficiency.

The importance of this need for intellectual effort cannot be overstated. It is so easy to think that a little human kindness is all that is needed, so easy to feel a warm glow at such a good intention. But the way forward is not easy. It is a hard way, demanding the best work that men can put into it. Kind hearts there must be; but clear heads are needed too.

(ii) *The fulfilment of the commandment must be an end in itself, not a mere means to an end.* My second general point is that good human relations in industry can only be surely founded on the treatment of each individual as a human personality whose welfare in the highest sense must be regarded as an end in itself. It is specially necessary to emphasize this point today when, in view of the desperate need to increase production, a new and intensified interest is being focused on all those conditions which affect industrial morale and people's will to work. This increased interest is all to the good, and one can see a bright side to the present emergency in that it has brought about such an awakening. But the interest once aroused must be of the right kind. If managers start now to take a human interest in the workers *merely* in order to improve production results, then they will be both wrong and unsuccessful. They will be wrong because regard for human beings should be seen as an end in itself. They will be unsuccessful because they will be found out. The whole industrial field is bedevilled with suspicions based on past memories. As a result, even the most honest attempts to improve human relations tend to be viewed with mistrust—either as dodges to get something extra out of the workers for the benefit of the profit-makers or as signs of a temporary mood 'produced by force of circumstances rather than a change of heart' (to quote words recently used to me by a trade union leader). If the success of genuine attempts is threatened by suspicion, bogus attempts will certainly fail.

It is so essential to visualize clearly what this treatment of the individual as an end in himself means that I want to say more about it. There is a passage in G. K. Chesterton's *Life of St. Francis of Assisi* which helps to illustrate my own understanding:

I have said that St. Francis deliberately did not see the wood for the trees. It is even more true that he deliberately did not see the mob for the men. What distinguishes this very genuine democrat from any mere demagogue is that he never either deceived or was deceived by the illusion of mass suggestion. Whatever his taste in monsters, he never saw the many-headed beast. He only saw the image of God multiplied and never monstrous. To him a man was always a man and did not disappear in a dense crowd any more than in a desert. He honoured all men; that is he not only loved but respected them all. What gave him his extraordinary personal power was this; that from the Pope to the beggar, from the Sultan of Syria in his pavilion to the ragged robber crawling out of the wood, there never was a man who looked into those brown burning eyes without being certain that Francis Bernardone was really interested in *him*; in his own inner individual life from the cradle to the grave; that he himself was being valued and taken seriously, and not merely added to the spoils of some social policy or the names in some clerical document.... And this was really and truly the only attitude that will appeal to that part of a man to which he wished to appeal. It cannot be done by giving gold or even bread. ... No plans or proposals or efficient rearrangements will give back to a broken man his respect and sense of speaking with an equal. One gesture will do it.

Now, I am not suggesting that we are likely to find men of the quality of St. Francis to fill the managerial posts in industry (or indeed that St. Francis with all his qualities would have made a good industrial manager); but in this particular matter I believe that the words which I have quoted give a pattern of conduct which we should set before us as an aim. And that surely is all that we can do. We shall not achieve perfection in any sphere of human activity or human relations; but we can set before ourselves a pattern of perfection as a goal toward which we must try to move. And for such a purpose the picture drawn by Chesterton is a great help—or at least so I have found it. And it is of value, too, in pointing to the dangers to guard against—in the implied warning against politicians or 'scientific management' experts or research workers, who may look at men merely as units 'to be added to the spoils of some social policy' or to provide data for hypotheses and conclusions in a research report.

(iii) *Objectives to be considered in the light of existing conditions.* There is a third point—a point of explanation—which I ought to include in these preliminary reflections. I propose to consider managerial responsibilities and human relations generally in terms of existing conditions. I am fully conscious that many among my audience may hold that it is impossible to work for a fulfilment of Christian principles without a revolutionary change in the whole economic system. I shall not shirk that issue; but I think it more helpful to start by trying to get a clear picture of results which it is desirable and practicable to achieve, expressed in terms of the arrangements which affect the daily lives of the men and women working in industry. Having got such a clear vision of the objectives, I can turn in a later passage to consider how far their attainment is affected by the general economic system.

The Interpretation of Christ's Second Commandment in Industrial Work

I come, therefore, now to my central question: How is Christ's second commandment to be interpreted in men's behaviour to each other in the daily working of industry? And I start with a man in a managerial position who asks himself this question. I have already said a good deal to indicate my own views. The necessary foundation for everything is what I may call the 'St. Francis' attitude of interest in each individual as a personality, expressed in sympathy and understanding. That shows the right spirit. But how, and with what end in view, is that spirit to express itself? I will give my own answer in very simple terms. If I, as a 'manager', am to 'love my neighbour as myself', my primary aim must surely be to do all that lies in my power, within the sphere of his activities which I can affect, to enable him to achieve for himself the sort of worldly life and opportunities of self-realization which, according to my own belief, I regard as a good life or 'happiness' in the highest sense, and which I accordingly seek for myself. Thus the essential question for me is how to make each worker's time within the factory something which fits in with a good life or happiness properly interpreted.

How, then, is this 'good life or happiness in the highest sense' to be interpreted? One's answer to this question must depend on one's own philosophy of life. Therefore I must state my own. This statement, if it is not to run to undue length, must be elementary, and I must concentrate on those aspects of a good life or happiness which can be influenced by industrial employment. I hope this will be remembered in case it is thought that I put undue emphasis on certain elements.

A Philosophy of Life

Briefly, my own philosophy of life is derived from Greek thought as modified by Christ's teaching. Looking at the question in terms of worldly life, I have found the most helpful starting point in the definition of the good life or happiness (*eudaimonia*) given at the beginning of Aristotle's

Ethics. He says it is to be found in *activity*—in doing well things that one can do well, and if one can do several things well then in doing those things which one can do best. He goes on to say that it is difficult, though not impossible, for any man to achieve this happiness, unless his life has an adequate material setting—'the stage properties for the play of life' he calls it—but this is no more than a condition of happiness, a means to an end, not an end in itself. Aristotle's exact words are 'activity according to a standard of excellence' (*energeia kat areten*) and to appreciate their meaning one must understand the Greek conception of excellence (*arete*), 'that conception which runs like a gold thread through the achievement of Greece'.[1] There is no exact English equivalent for the Greek word *arete*, but 'excellence' roughly indicates the meaning. It is a conception of excellence as something to be sought in every sphere and activity, a conception that everything, whether it be a human faculty or an object of art or utility, has its own true form of excellence which should be striven for as an end in itself. The business of life, the Greeks thought, is to seek the highest and make the most of whatever man is or does.

There may be better ends [writes Sir Richard Livingstone] but this is not a mean one, and it is simple, intelligible, convincing and practical. It leaves money in the right place. It is a perpetual challenge in hours of doubt, weariness, slackness and pessimism. It is a philosophy consistent with Christianity.

But it needs to be transformed by Christian teaching and fitted in to quite a different scale of values. Plato and Aristotle thought that reason was the noblest thing in man and therefore that the highest life was the life of reason lived by poets and philosophers and men of science. The

[1] I take these words from Sir Richard Livingstone (*Education for a World Adrift*, p. 92), and in the sentences which follow I have used much of his wording. I find it difficult to avoid doing this, because he has put so supremely well what I want to say. He and I read for Greats together at Oxford, and our thoughts were moulded in the same form, except perhaps that I rely rather more on Aristotle than he does.

idea that manual work could be an ennobling activity was quite excluded by Greek philosophy. Aristotle even says that true happiness 'cannot be found by man in any form of practical life, no not even in the fullest and freest exercise possible of the moral virtues, not in the life of the citizen or the great soldier or statesman, but only in the contemplative life'.[2] The Greek idea is thus unsatisfying for Christians in two ways: it is too narrow, and it is too cold and intellectual. It needs to be widened by the inclusion of every kind of work or activity, and to be warmed by the Christian conception of love. No man can fulfil himself properly, even as an individual, except as a member of a community. He must have relations with his fellow men, and these must be inspired by love in the Christian sense. In short, the Greek idea needs to be transformed by St. Paul's conception of the highest virtue and human excellence as explained in the thirteenth chapter of the First Epistle to the Corinthians.

But though I believe profoundly that St. Paul's words show us the 'more excellent way' and that, without the spirit of love or charity which he preaches, all 'excellences' in wordly activities lose their virtue, none the less when I try to answer the particular question of how to make industrial work an element of a good life—or indeed any other question about practical conduct in our modern industrial society—the Greek conception helps to point the way. The 'golden thread' needs to be woven into a new fabric. Such an idea is certainly not inconsistent with Christ's teaching. Not only does His parable of the talents show His recognition of its value, but a true interpretation of His first commandment seems to me to give a new significance to the Greek idea. The commandment to love God 'with all thy *mind*' must surely mean, among other things, that all kinds of work, whether intellectual or manual, should be done in a spirit of dedication to

[2] Professor J. A. Smith, Introduction to Chase's translation of the *Ethics*.

God and therefore done just as well as the doer can possibly do it. Nothing but the best of which a man is capable can be good enough if the work is seen as service to God.

There is one other important point which I must add in considering the conception of activity. This, if it is to be a satisfying element in a good life, must be *free* activity. There must be sufficient scope for the exercise of personal self-expression and personal responsibility.

The Three Foundation Stones for a Good Life. Reducing all my reflections to simple practical terms, my belief is that the conception of good work well done, in conditions of liberty, and in an atmosphere of human love and comradeship, gives a working guide to what is needed to provide the foundations for happiness in the worldly life. At least I see these as the three foundation stones; and, when one who has to direct the work of his fellow men in industrial employment seeks an answer to the question of how he is to behave as a Christian to them, my answer would be that he should do everything possible to enable them to find these three foundation stones for their lives.

Some Further Reflections on Activity and Work. It is by considering what this means in terms of practical conduct that I propose to follow out my subject. But before I do that I want to say something more in order to expound and reinforce my conception of the importance of active work as an essential element in the sort of life that God meant men to live in this world. First of all there is one's own experience in life. I can speak with certainty of my own experience, but I feel little doubt that it must be yours also. As I see it, nobody can be happy in this life unless he feels that he is doing useful work. There is no more certain cause of misery and demoralization than inactivity, aimlessness, the feeling that you are not wanted. The truth of this was surely brought out vividly by the effects of unemployment in the inter-war years, effects so well depicted in plays like *Love on the Dole*, in novels like *How Green was My Valley*, or in social studies such as the Pilgrim Trust Report on *Men without Work*. These show on the negative side the misery of being without work; but it is easy too to find evidence on the positive side of the satisfaction achieved by ordinary people from the sense of useful work accomplished. As I am writing these words, I have before me a report by a research team on an attitude survey in three Royal Ordnance Factories, from which I quote the following paragraph:

Many, though not all, of those who spoke of money as an incentive also mentioned other reasons for wanting to work. A considerable proportion of both men and women said that they liked working hard for its own sake, that they were used to doing so, or that time dragged if there were not plenty of work. Some typical comments from the men were: 'I like working hard because I'm used to it. It's the way I was born. At twelve years old I used to walk four miles to work at 4 a.m. and got 7s. 6d. a week'; and 'I like working. I must work. If I were out of work I might as well be dead. Nine out of ten men are satisfied if they're working.' The women also made such remarks as 'I like to work hard. I've worked ever since I was twelve and it's been a pleasure', and 'I feel better when I'm working hard. My happiest days were when I was at home with three small children, but now they're grown up and don't want me any more and all I have is my work to keep me occupied.' Some operatives also made the somewhat similar but more positive comment that they derived satisfaction from the knowledge that they had done a good day's work, and others spoke of working hard because of their interest in the job, because they felt masters of it, or because, more simply, they felt happy when doing it; many of these comments were very similar to those already quoted as reasons given for liking jobs.

These are very ordinary remarks, hardly worth quoting perhaps. Yet I do quote them because I think we so often concentrate attention on signs of disturbance or trouble, and thus fail to take account of the flow of ordinary people's lives.

I turn from these thoughts of ordinary people to the opinions of psychologists. I will give no more than two quotations which indicate their approach.[3] Here is a quotation from Freud:

Laying stress upon the importance of work has a greater effect than any other technique of living in the direction of binding the individual more closely to reality; in his work he is at least securely attached to a part of reality, the human community. Work is no less valuable for the opportunity it and the human relations connected with it provide for a very considerable discharge of libidinal component impulses, narcissistic, aggressive and even erotic, than because it is indispensable for subsistence and justified existence in a society. The daily work of earning a livelihood affords particular satisfaction when it has been selected by free choice, i.e. when through sublimation it enables use to be made of existing inclinations, or instinctual impulses that have retained their strength, or are more intense than usual for constitutional reasons (*Civilization and Its Discontents*).

Jung expresses a similar point of view:

The best liberation is through regular work. Work, however, is salvation only when it is a free act and has in itself nothing of infantile compulsion (*Psychology of the Unconscious*).

I turn next to the views of philosophers. I have already quoted Aristotle. Let me turn from him to a philosopher of a very different type and era—Bernard Shaw. I have always liked this well-known passage from his Preface to *Man and Superman*:

This is the true joy in life, the being used for a purpose recognized by yourself as a mighty one; the being thoroughly worn out before you are thrown on the scrap heap; the being a force of Nature instead of a feverish little clod of ailment and grieving, complaining that the world will not devote itself to making you happy. And the only real tragedy in life is the being used by personally minded men for purposes which you recognize to be base. All the rest is mere misfortune or mortality. This alone is misery.

[3] For a fuller discussion, see *Free Expression in Industry*, by J. J. Gillespie, p. 72.

These words may seem rather grandiose in relation to the humdrum tasks of daily work in industry; but they throw light on the essential points—the joy in work as a creative activity, the evil of treating people as instruments for purposes which they cannot understand and recognize as worthy.

Finally, I turn for support to what has been said by leading religious thinkers. I can find that in some words of the late William Temple, spoken with his characteristic readiness to come down into the market-place and talk the language of ordinary men. I vividly remember him, in the course of an after-dinner group discussion, saying: 'It is a mistake to suppose that God is interested solely in religion. God is a worker getting on with his job. He gave man the joy of creation so that he might share his work with Him.' Or I can look to another profound and helpful religious thinker, Nicolas Berdyaev, to find this same view expressed in less popular language. One of the main themes in his book, *Freedom and the Spirit*, is that to be human is to be endowed with freedom and summoned to creativity: 'Because of the very nature of God Himself who is infinite love and the cause of the divine plan of creation itself, the Kingdom of God can be realized only through man's co-operation and the participation of creation itself.'[4]

Is it too much to regard these high conceptions as applicable to the ordinary daily tasks of workers in manufacturing industry? Surely not. At any rate, I believe that they are relevant to my subject and that the idea that men (and all men, however humble their tasks) are called on to play a part with God in creation, seen as an ever-continuing process, is a fruitful and inspiring one.

Two Practical Questions. But I must turn back from inspiring visions of this kind to the practical details of

[4] *Freedom and the Spirit*, p. 197, quoted in *Nicolas Berdyaev. Freedom in God*, by E. L. Allen (Hodder and Stoughton).

working life; and at this point it is appropriate to examine two questions which will doubtless be in the minds of many of those who have followed my argument so far. The basic idea from which I started was that *activity*—the active exercise of a man's best faculties—is a main foundation stone for happiness or a good life. But—and this is the first question—is this activity necessarily to be identified with a man's breadwinning work? And if so—as the second question—can breadwinning work in modern industry provide creative activity of a kind which could fulfil my purpose? My answer to the first question is that I certainly do not regard breadwinning work as necessarily providing the whole of a man's soul-satisfying activity. A full and happy life should include many more activities than that—activities based on a wide range of family and social obligations and leisure interests of all kinds. But what I do want to argue, and argue most strongly, is that there can be no satisfactory form of industrial society (and ours must now be such a society) if the great numbers who are engaged in industrial employment and all its accessory economic activities, can find happiness only in escape from their breadwinning work. And the essential point in all that I have to say is that the *greatest need of our modern industrial society is to make industrial employment something which is, and is seen as, an essential part of a satisfactory human life (individual and social) and not as a cause of conflict or an evil burden to be escaped from or reduced as far as possible.* Can this need be met? It is in this form that I have to answer the second question. And it is with that limited question and not with the wider question of the whole foundation for a good life that I am essentially concerned in this lecture.

Industrial Work as Part of a Satisfactory Life. As a preliminary to giving my answer to this question, it is necessary to examine more closely the meaning of some of the words which I have used. What exactly is the

significance of the objective of making industrial employment 'an essential part of a satisfactory human life'?
There has recently been much discussion on this subject
which makes me feel it important to clarify one's ideas
and to keep a balance between extreme views on either
side. On the one hand, there is what I regard as the
unduly pessimistic view of those who say that the conditions of modern industry, with its mass-production
methods and the breakdown of skilled craftsman's jobs
into repetitive, unskilled, machine-minding operations,
have made it impossible for the bulk of manual workers
to find in their daily work a soul-satisfying activity. On
the other hand, there has been a tendency among certain
writers to preach too facile a doctrine of 'make work the
happy activity'. I believe, indeed, that there are ways in
which modern industry can offer opportunities of new
kinds of interest to offset the loss of the individual craftsman's interest. But it is foolish to minimize the difficulties.
To a great extent these may be reduced with the guidance
of better knowledge, and there is need for further study on
many aspects of the problem: how particular jobs affect
different people, what proportion of drudgery is tolerable
or even desirable as a sort of 'roughage' in our spiritual
and mental diet, how jobs and machines can be designed
with better regard for the human beings who have to do
and operate them, and so on.

All these are relevant questions on which I hope to
throw light in later passages. But when all is said and
done, one must recognize that there will always be a great
range of variation in the satisfaction that can be got from
different classes of work, as well as in the need or capacity
for this kind of satisfaction among different individuals.
It may range from the joy of the creative artist or scientist
to the mere comfortable feeling of doing a useful job which
earns daily bread for the doer and his family. Appreciat-
ing these differences in the opportunities offered by

different kinds of work, one can say that they ought to be offset in various ways; for example, the less the creative satisfaction in the work itself the greater is the need for supplementing it with satisfactions in comradeship, in understanding the common purpose of the working team, and in the use of leisure. But I think there is more in the problem than that. I think one must recognize that there are two aspects in work: first, the *duty*, as a condition of self-respect, to perform a breadwinning task for oneself and one's family; secondly, the *opportunity* to achieve happiness through creative activity. It is only a small fraction of humanity which can be fortunate enough perfectly to combine the two (i.e. to find their full happiness through the exercise of their best faculties in their bread-winning work), and I have come to feel that it is danger-ous and intrinsically wrong to encourage expectations that anyone has a right to expect such a perfect com-bination. The *duty* element must be preserved. To fulfil it can be seen as a condition of happiness, but should not be identified with it.

This leads me to the conclusion that the right way to put this point is to say that at the very lowest industrial work should be so handled that it can be regarded as a dignified activity, a necessity of nature, a condition of self-respect; *not* as something which is a definite evil either in itself or because the burden is unnecessarily increased by the incompetence or indifference of 'management' or by the greed of shareholders and financiers. My thesis in this lecture is that to make industrial work a satisfying activity in this sense is not too difficult, provided that the negative and obstructive influences which create dis-satisfactions can be removed. How this is to be done in terms of practical arrangements is what I have now to discuss: but before I pass to this discussion there are three points I must add in order to complete my explanation of the basic conception.

The first is that when I state a conception of work which 'at the very lowest' ought to be possible, I do not imply that those who carry managerial responsibilities ought to be satisfied with this minimum. On the contrary, they should be seeking in every possible way both to increase the positive satisfactions in work and also to ensure that industrial employment is so handled that it fits in with a satisfactory social setting for people's lives outside their working hours.

My second point is that when one considers practical measures it is necessary to take account not only of the activity of work, but also of the other two elements which I have included in my 'three foundation stones' for a satisfying life—freedom and a setting of human love and comradeship. As to conditions of freedom, when people talk about that today they are generally thinking of political freedom. I am concerned with what is equally important—freedom in work. And this means not merely freedom in the choice of a job, but, what I believe matters still more, freedom in the sense that a man should have a chance to express himself in his work, have some share in saying how it is to be done and not be treated as a mere automatic piece of machinery which 'is not paid to think'. Then as to the setting of human love and comradeship, one of the most important aims of organization (on which I shall have much to say in later passages) must be to create working groups in which real comradeship is possible.

My third point is a reminder that, although I shall start by considering what 'management' can and should do in its relations with the workers, this is only one of three aspects of human relations in industry, and that the efforts of management cannot succeed unless the workers respond and unless they are ready to develop the right relations with each other.

THE PRACTICAL IMPLICATIONS OF MANAGERIAL
RESPONSIBILITY

I come now to the question of what practical arrangements will help to attain the general objective of making industrial work an essential part of a satisfactory human life.

The General Objective Analysed

It may be helpful at the start to attempt to analyse this general objective into component parts in terms of conditions to be satisfied. I should say that conditions ought to be such that each worker (i) can feel that he has an individual responsibility for his job and that he has some freedom for expressing himself in it; (ii) can feel that he is working as a member of a team with a sense of comradeship and joint responsibility; (iii) can understand the place of his work in the total purpose of the factory and feel that this purpose is not unworthy; (iv) can work at tasks which give the satisfaction of skill in performance and of effort accomplished without overtaxing strain; (v) can be satisfied that the methods of production and the general policy in his factory are such that he can get a fair run at his work, and that he is not being 'messed about' or prevented from getting full value from his working effort because of avoidable inefficiencies on the part of 'management'; and, finally (vi), can be satisfied that the payment for his work is both adequate for his needs and also fair. Of course, I do not say that every worker consciously thinks out a list like this for himself; but I believe that in practice there must be a fair degree of fulfilment of all these conditions if there is to be attainment of the main purpose that I have indicated.

Functional Efficiency a Primary Responsibility for Management

Taking this list of conditions, what must a 'manager' do to fulfil them? My own first answer to this is that he must be efficient at his job. He ought to do all in his power to make himself efficient, and he ought not to hold on to a responsible job if he is not. I have already said (p. 19) that I see this as an ethical obligation—as part of the service *with the mind* which is enjoined in Christ's two commandments. I want now to explain the practical significance of this more fully. My essential idea is that it is not enough for a 'manager' to be human and kind-hearted: these qualities he must have, but their exercise cannot mitigate the crime of failure in his primary functional duty. Now, I hope no one will think that I am one who would sacrifice all the warm human values to a cold mechanical idea of 'efficiency'. On the contrary, what I am pleading for is that the warm human values should not be sacrificed to *inefficiency*. How often in the past have those who have sought to get more humane conditions in industry been met with the excuse: 'Our business cannot afford such luxuries; we should be ruined and have to close down, and then the workers would be the worst sufferers.' How often has that been the plea of inefficiency. How often has it been proved in practice that a well-run business *could* afford them. I do not deny that there is a danger if productivity is seen as the sole objective, and I often think that American methods, of which we are nowadays hearing so much, have tended to be inhuman and to sacrifice the man to the machine. But I believe that this danger can be avoided and that is why it is so important to see ethical obligations and economic purposes in their right relationship. Everyone in business is involved, not only in economic activities, but also in human relations, and for the latter he must take account, not only of economic, but also of ethical purposes, the chief of which should be to ensure that the industrial activities for which he is responsible afford the basis of good lives for the workers. He must reconcile the two purposes. I do not believe that a man who can only make his business profitable by neglecting his ethical obligations is a good business man or that he can be permanently successful. That does not mean that he is in business 'for charity'. His job in business is to conduct his enterprise profitably; but, to be really efficient, he must be able to make profits without ignoring ethical considerations.

Efficiency as a Basis for Confidence and Co-operation. That is one aspect of the matter; but there is another which is equally important. I have included in my list of conditions that the 'worker' must be satisfied that the methods of production and the general policy of the factory are such that he can get a fair run at this work, and that he is not being 'messed about' or prevented from getting full value from his working effort because of avoidable inefficiencies on the part of management. I am sure that this is something of great importance—an importance which will steadily increase as the level of general education improves and as the trade union leaders take an increasing interest in the improvement of productivity (which they ought to do and which they are now doing). Confidence in the efficiency of management is an essential condition for the spirit of co-operation on which the future of our nation as well as the happiness of individual workers depend.

I could give many practical illustrations of the importance of this. Here is one statement which I quote because it has come to me just as I was writing these words. It occurs in an interesting report on a comparative study of productivity carried out in a number of factories by the Research Association of the Boot and Shoe Industry:

The Survey Team gained the impression that as compared with conditions in some of the other factories there tended to be a happier atmosphere where productivity and quality were high. This may be because high productivity is associated with freedom from muddle, delays and frustration, and tends to occur only under orderly and satisfying working conditions. On the basis of the observations made during this survey, it is the opinion of the authors that high productivity can be obtained without imposing any undue strain on the operatives and without requiring them to race through the work to the detriment of craftsmanship or pride in the job, and that increases in productivity bring higher wages without necessarily increasing the feeling on the part of the operatives that they are 'slaves to the machines'.

Efficiency to be seen as an End in Itself. There is yet one more aspect of this matter to which I must refer before I leave it. I have been speaking of functional efficiency in a manager as a means to certain ends affecting the workers; but it must also, according to my doctrine, be seen as an end in itself. That follows from what I have said about work being carried out in a spirit of dedication to God and about the Greek conception of 'excellence' (pp. 23, 24). I refer to this again now because I want to make the point that this conception should be applied to industrial activities. There should be an ideal of 'excellence' in this sense which everyone engaged in industry should set before himself, and which is just as honourable an ideal, just as much worth seeking for its own sake, as excellence in the arts or literature or statesmanship or any other human activity.

PRACTICAL ARRANGEMENTS

Having emphasized the overriding importance and ethical significance of functional efficiency among industrial managers, I must now turn to discuss some of the practical arrangements through which this efficiency is to express itself. In a lecture like this it is clearly impossible to give an exhaustive account of all that is involved in the functions of management. My discussion must therefore be a limited one, calling attention only to the main features and looking at these from the point of view of one who is considering how an industry can be run so as to provide soul-satisfying employment for those who work in it.

I propose to arrange what I have to say under five main headings:

(i) *Form of organization.*
(ii) *Working conditions and industrial health.*
(iii) *Arrangements for 'fitting the man to the job and the job to the man',* which includes methods of selection, training, promotion, work planning, and plant design.
(iv) *Arrangements for the division of the proceeds of the work,* covering methods of settling pay, profit sharing, etc.
(v) *Methods of communication and joint consultation.*

This list by no means covers the whole field; but a consideration of its headings will enable me to make the points which chiefly need attention in connexion with my subject. The headings are not arranged in order of importance—certainly the last in the list is not the least important; but I have chosen this order as a matter of convenience.

Form of Organization

The form of organization is vitally important. There are four main needs: first there must be a clear line of authority, so that every individual knows for what and to whom he is responsible. Without this there can be neither adequate achievement in terms of results for the concern as a whole nor satisfactory working opportunities for the individuals employed in it. The second need is to ensure that arrangements are such that every decision can be taken at the level where it can be most rapidly and effectively taken—that nothing should have to be unnecessarily held up for reference to a higher level. A third need is to provide for the maintenance of personal relationships and for avoiding the dangers of remote impersonal control. Every individual, at whatever level he may be in the organization, should feel that he has someone in the line of authority above him who is in personal contact with him, who understands him as a person, who can appreciate his work, who can listen to his suggestions about it, and who is so placed that he can ensure that proper attention is given by 'management' to these matters.

The fourth need (which I can conveniently mention as a matter of organization, though it has wider significance) is that the production processes should be so arranged as to allow for the formation of effective working groups. In fact, I believe that the most important problem in modern industrial organization is to discover in each case what is the effective working group. That should be the unit on which to build. Each group should be large enough to accomplish a recognizably distinct component part in the total operations of the factory, and small enough to give its individual members the sense of personal comradeship and the feeling that each has within his own group a significant part to play. The organization must then provide for the collaboration of these 'primary' groups in larger groupings, and so on until at the topmost level all the threads are brought together for the factory as a whole. That is, no doubt, an over-simplified picture, but it indicates the right pattern for an organization which can combine the power to follow out a central guiding policy with a measure of decentralization which permits a wide exercise of initiative right out to the perimeter, and can give to each individual a feeling that, as a member of his own working group, he can exercise an influence, not only on the way in which his own particular job is handled, but also to some extent at least on the central guiding policy. It is through arrangements of this kind that a true co-operating community can be built up, and that the significance of each individual personality can be preserved from being lost even in the largest organizations. It is by such arrangements, too, that opportunities can be created for new satisfactions and new forms of interest for workers in modern industry. The spirit of what I have said has been well expressed by Edmund Burke.

To be attached to the subdivision, to love the little platoon we belong to in society, is the first principle (the term as it were) of public affections.

All the four needs that I have mentioned are being felt with increasing intensity today owing to the tendency toward ever larger units. All, moreover, arise in a new and acute form in the case of the nationalized industries. The outstanding problem throughout industry, nationalized and private alike, is how to achieve the central direction which is necessary for the fulfilment of national policies and for achieving a concerted national effort, without creating overcentralization and a degree of rigidity which must hamper individual responsibility, enterprise, and initiative.

Many books and articles are now being written on these matters and there is a growing appreciation of what is involved and of the need for further study and experiment. I cannot attempt a comprehensive examination and must be content with the sketch of the four main points which I have given. There is, however, one further point which I wish to add, since I am trying now to give my conception of the duties of those who carry managerial responsibilities. This is that, as means for effecting continuous improvement in organization and methods, the leaders of industrial firms should do everything possible to ensure that the fullest advantage is taken of the lessons of experience. This means not only studying their own experience for themselves, but also giving others the opportunity to profit from their lessons. Many devices are today being tried out by progressive industrial firms, and much practical experience is being gained. I do not think full advantage is being derived from this experience. I think all firms should do more to maintain accurate objective records of the evolutionary development of their organization, and should publish their 'case histories' and the lessons to be derived from them. The maintenance of full case-history records would make the experience of each firm more fruitful for itself; the publication of the records would make it of value to the whole community. The pursuit of both purposes should be seen as ethical obligations. I want particularly to emphasize the latter. Secretiveness in industry has been one of our national shortcomings, and, as a result, the country has been failing to get the full benefit of experience which is available within our own shores. It is the fashion just now to look to America for lessons, and certainly in the matter of frank disclosure by industrial firms of their own methods and experience American practice has been better than our own. There have recently been welcome signs of a move toward more informative statements by some of the leading British industrial concerns; but there is need for this move to go much farther. This is a form of Christian generosity which should be widely practised.

Working Conditions and Industrial Health

Working conditions and industrial health may seem to be straightforward matters; but they are very important and their full implications are not always appreciated. Health, both physical and mental, even if it is not to be regarded as an end in itself, is a vitally important condition for a good life, and if industrial managers are to take account of Christ's second commandment they must do everything possible to ensure that the work that they have to direct can be carried on in conditions consistent with the maintenance of good health. This involves much more than the obvious duty of taking all possible preventive and curative measures to reduce the effects of what may be described as 'straight industrial diseases'. Minor ailments, accidents, and mental health have all to be considered. And beyond this, the general conception should be the positive one of seeking all possible means to promote health, rather than the mere negative one of preventing disease.

Occupational Diseases. There is much to be learned from past history in these matters and our record is not one of which, as a Christian industrial nation, we can be proud. Even in the case of so obvious a duty as countering the straight industrial diseases there has been serious neglect. It is only in recent years that anything like an adequate attempt has been started to study the causes and effects of these diseases. An instructive illustration is the work of the Medical Research Council's Pneumoconiosis Research Unit in South Wales. Here is a disease which has caused great misery and many tragedies, and which has had far-reaching social effects.[5] But it was not until the last few years that the resources of science were adequately directed to its investigation. One has only to study the work in this case, or what is being done on a smaller scale in the case of another coalminers' disease (nystagmus) in Durham, to realize how much there is to learn and how much to be done. And these two projects reveal something more. They bring out the value of the scientific approach: they show how disinterested scientists, studying matters which deeply affect men's lives, can overcome the suspicions to which I referred in an earlier passage (p. 19), and establish relations of sympathy and understanding with the workers.

I am tempted to dwell further on the coalmining industry as affording other illustrations that are relevant to the theme of this lecture. One way to get a conception

5 Pneumoconiosis means literally 'dust in the lungs' and denotes a form of pulmonary dust disease suffered by coalminers which has been specially prevalent in South Wales. Men suffering from this disease were first given compensation in 1928. In South Wales between 1931 and 1938 over 19,000 were certified under the Workmen's Compensation Act.

of what a Christian industrialist ought to do is to study examples of what he ought not to do; and, if anyone wants a clear picture of things which ought not to be done, he can find it in the story of coalmining. Let him, for example, go round Durham and Northumberland, and see the vast palatial mansions which coal-owners in the nineteenth century built for themselves and contrast their past purposes with their present use as rehabilitation centres. Until quite recently, such centres did not exist, in spite of the heavy incidence of accidents in coalmining. Today a house built in Victorian times for a single rich family serves as a rehabilitation centre for a whole mining county.

Accidents. This last illustration takes me into the field of accidents—a very important matter when one is considering industrial health. Not nearly enough attention has been devoted in the past to studying their causes and incidence. The safety regulations as officially prescribed and worked by Government inspectors do not and cannot provide all the protection that is required. Employers have a heavy responsibility in this matter. Few people, I believe, realize how much time is lost or how morale is affected by what may be described as minor accidents. In the case of coalmining, to which I have already referred, the incidence of accidents (and, I might add, the fear of accidents) is a major factor. Omitting the specific and serious types of accident which are reportable to the Inspector of Mines under the Coal Mines Act, it can be said that in every year roughly one miner out of every four working underground suffers a 'compensatable' accident, that is to say, an accident serious enough to keep him three days or more away from work.[6] Minor accidents

[6] The figures officially published by the Ministry of Fuel and Power for 1946 show that 150,000 compensatable accidents were sustained by 525,000 men working underground. If one considers 'recorded' accidents (that is to say, those which were recorded at the pit-head, but do not lead to a compensatable absence), I believe it would be fair to put them at something

also represent an important field for study in manufacturing industries—especially the light engineering industries. Here again some interesting work has been going on in the last years under the sponsorship of the Medical Research Council. A survey in the Birmingham area indicates that in the average light engineering factory from 7 to 10 per cent of the workers injure themselves daily, and from 1 to $1\frac{1}{2}$ per cent report with injuries to the factory surgery. Of these about two-thirds are cuts, lacerations, or puncture wounds. In the year, a number equivalent to 3 per cent of the factory workers have injuries causing them to be off work for more than three days, the mean loss of time for injury being some twenty-four to thirty-one days.[7] I quote these figures as illustrating the kind of things in the field of industrial health and working conditions to which management should devote attention. The study of the incidence, causes, cure, and treatment of minor accidents is an important responsibility of management. The mere fact that management is paying attention to this kind of responsibility can be taken as a sign of a human interest in the workers and can have an appreciable effect on general morale in a factory.

Mental Health. I pass from the subjects of diseases and accidents to that of mental health. This has always been of importance, and I believe it is a characteristic of modern conditions that its importance is likely to get greater. The increasing pace of industry—and indeed of life generally—involves increasing nervous strain. Also perhaps in some ways human nature is becoming less

like two and a half times as many as the 'compensatable' accidents. These figures take no account of all those accidents such as cuts, bruises, lacerations, etc., which are not recorded, but which are numerous.

[7] These and other interesting figures are given in an article, 'Industrial Injuries', by Dr. J. P. Bull in the *British Medical Bulletin*, 1950, 7, 69. The work of the Medical Research Council Unit (of which Dr. Bull is a member) has led to the development of some effective and easily applied dressings for minor injuries, the use of which has greatly reduced the time lost from work.

tough. But, however that may be, this part of the field merits increasing attention. The report of a recent survey, promoted by the Industrial Health Research Board of the Medical Research Council, gave striking confirmation of the importance of the psychological factor. This report[8] showed that, in the factories examined, over 25 per cent of all sickness absence was due to neurosis; that 10 per cent of all the workers examined (9 per cent of the men and 13 per cent of the women) had suffered from definite and disabling neurotic illness during the six months covered by the investigation; and that a further 20 per cent (19·2 per cent of the men and 23 per cent of the women) had experienced minor forms of neurosis. This record was based on an examination of 3,000 workers selected as a random sample from 30,000 employed in a group of thirteen light engineering factories. Although it was carried out during the war the investigators reported that 'during the period of survey . . . few of the conditions notably peculiar to war were operative', so that it gave a fair idea of general conditions. It was not the purpose of the inquiry to show how neurotic illness can best be alleviated, but the report says that it is 'implicit in its findings that measures tantamount to good welfare and social work *both within and outside the factory* would be beneficial in alleviating and preventing neuroses'.

It may be of interest to take another illustration which confirms the importance of giving attention to mental health. As I was preparing this lecture, it happened that a friend in New York sent me a paper setting out a research programme for 1950 planned by Columbia University under the direction of its then head, General Eisenhower:

General Eisenhower [says the report] has taken the leadership in initiating a comprehensive study of the Conservation of Human Resources. He has been concerned with what he terms the wastage of the nation's most valuable asset.

[8] *The Incidence of Neurosis among Factory Workers*, Industrial Health Research Board Report No. 90 (1947).

As illustrative of the areas with which the research is concerned, the following points (*inter alia*) were made:

1. At the present time more than half of all the hospital beds of the country are filled with patients who are suffering from mental disorders. For instance, in the state of New York, the single largest item in the State budget is devoted to the Department of Mental Hygiene, which is now spending considerably in excess of $100 million annually. Particularly ominous is the fact that the total case load continues to mount, so that at the present time approximately one out of every 150 citizens is in a mental institution.

2. The costs of mental breakdown in military life have also been most severe. During the past war two million men were rejected for service for emotional or mental reasons. At the present time approximately 500,000 veterans are in receipt of pensions from the United States Government because they were discharged from the Service for an emotional disability. Almost half of the beds in veterans' hospitals are devoted to ex-soldiers who have suffered a mental breakdown, and the cost of caring for one such veteran during the course of his natural lifetime may mount to as much as $80,000.

I have referred to the Industrial Health Research Board report and to the Columbia University Research Programme because the conditions which they reveal help to make clear the importance of 'mental health'.[9] The former report, too, brings out the point that it is important to study, not only how the work within the factory is affecting each individual, but also how the factory work fits in with the workers' external environment (domestic and social) and how the latter may affect attitudes to work. Strain caused by factory work,

---

[9] Its importance is further illustrated by the statistics of general conditions in the United Kingdom. See the following quotations from the Ministry of Health Report for 1949:

Other investigators, not only psychiatrists, have estimated that 30 to 50 per cent of all cases seen by general practitioners and in general clinics are neurotic or have a large neurotic component (p. 130).

Few appreciate the size or importance of the problem of mental illness. Perhaps it can best be illustrated by the fact that at the end of 1948 there were in England and Wales approximately 200,000 beds for mental illness and mental defectives and 315,000 beds for all other types of illness (p. 133).

either because of the nature of the work itself or because the claims of the work are in conflict with outside influences, may be a cause of neurosis or 'emotional disability', while, conversely, work which suits the worker and provides the chance for the healthy exercise of his faculties can be a powerful antidote to mental or emotional disorders caused by outside factors. It is one of the duties of those who direct industrial enterprise to do everything possible to see that this harmony is ensured and that outside conditions are taken into account.

The Creation of Positive Health. This leads me to my last point under the heading of Industrial Health, the point that the aim should be essentially constructive—the creation of positive health—and not merely the treatment and prevention of diseases and accidents. As a means to this end, I myself believe that a whole-time works medical officer should be employed and have a place in the management team of every large-scale factory. (Smaller units could combine to employ a whole-time officer.) I say this not only because I believe a medical officer of the right type is particularly well placed to make valuable human contacts, but also because I think that nothing should be done in the way of settling the design and lay-out of plant or the introduction of new processes without taking into account the effect on the health of the workers. And it follows from what I have already said that 'health' for this purpose should be widely interpreted and that account should be taken of psychological as well as physical reactions.

The last paragraphs conveniently lead on to my next heading:

Fitting the Job to the Man and the Man to the Job
This double heading covers a wide range of subjects. Its two sides are interdependent, but each has its own distinct list of problems.

'*Fitting the job to the man*' involves study of such matters as the arrangement of the processes of production, and their subdivision into individual tasks; the design of working equipment with regard to the human beings that have to operate it; the conditions influencing the effective use of such equipment (lighting, temperature, etc.); 'motion study' as a means of discovering how a particular result can be achieved most accurately, rapidly, and with the least fatigue. The expression 'human engineering' can be conveniently used to designate the main part of the work covered by this heading.

'*Fitting the man to the job*' covers methods of selection and training, and involves the study of personal aptitudes —not only the differing individual aptitudes among normal people, but also the distinctive aptitudes of special classes such as juveniles, elderly persons, or persons with various limiting disabilities.

These are vitally important matters, the proper handling of which can have a profound effect on the degree of satisfaction to be got out of industrial work. They are matters too in regard to which there is special scope for scientific research, and as I have said in an earlier passage (p. 30) there is need for more knowledge on many aspects of what may be described as the psychology of work. An important point to note in this connexion is that scientific research work cannot realize its full value unless those who are concerned with the practical conduct of industry take an active interest both in promoting the research and also in applying the knowledge which it produces. Here is one of the chief responsibilities for industrial leaders, including in that term not only the management side, but also trade union leaders.

I cannot attempt to deal comprehensively with these subjects and must content myself with giving a few illustrations to indicate their significance.

Fitting the Job to the Man. 'Fitting the job to the man'

can be considered in two different aspects—the arrangement of the job and the design of machines.

As to the arrangement of the job, an important question is how far it is right to break down work into separate simplified operations. (The making of a waistcoat, for example, may be divided into seventeen separate operations, each performed repetitively by different individuals.) It is being questioned now whether, even from a production point of view, it is right to go beyond a certain point in this process of breaking down, since more than what is gained by making each job simpler may be lost by the psychological effect on the worker of dull monotony. Obviously, from the point of view of its effects on human satisfactions, this question is still more important. This is the kind of subject on which more research is required; and it may be of interest to note that a study of the 'unit of work' is one of the research projects sponsored by the Panel on Human Factors Affecting Industrial Productivity[10] of which I have been Chairman.

Next let me turn to the subject of designing machines with regard to the human beings who have to operate them. This too is a subject on which scientific research is clearly desirable. Not only the speed and accuracy with which work can be done, but also the satisfaction of the worker through a sense of fruitful effort achieved by harmonious, unstrained motions, can be greatly affected by the way in which machinery is designed—the arrangements for the workers' posture, the methods of control, the design of dials and indicators, etc. It is a curious reflection on human conduct to note that it has required the exigencies of war to direct attention to these matters. On active service there can be no evasion of realities. If complicated modern instruments of war are to be effectively handled by their human operators, then, in their

[10] This was one of the four Panels of the Government's Committee on Industrial Productivity.

design, account must be taken of how the receptor and effector impulses of the human body work. It is necessary, therefore, to get scientists to study these and to apply their knowledge in designing such things as the machinery for the laying and firing of guns, the driving seat of a tank, or the arrangement of the instruments on the control board of the aircraft pilot. And it so happens that the research work that has been done in this field of 'human engineering' has been stimulated mainly by the Service Departments. Now, however, the work is being extended into the field of manufacturing industry. The Medical Research Council, through its Industrial Health Research Board, is interested in it, and some of the research projects sponsored by the Panel on Human Factors, to which I have already referred, have been concerned with matters of this kind.

To introduce a lighter note, I was amused recently to note that a professor of anatomy (who has been engaged on work of this kind for the Medical Research Council) was brought in to advise on the design of the seats in the reconstructed House of Commons. To secure the comfort of the listening audience in Parliament is no doubt a laudable objective; but I could wish that comparable attention had been given long ago to securing a comfortable position for the thousands who are operating machine tools in British industry.

Fitting the Man to the Job. What I have been saying indicates some of the things which are involved in 'fitting the job to the man'. The complementary heading of 'fitting the man to the job' can have even wider scope and significance. Selection and training are matters of vital importance. Under both heads the methods hitherto practised in British industry as a whole have been far too haphazard and unsystematic. Selection covers the initial placing of individuals in the 'rank and file' jobs, and also the choice of particular individuals for promotion.

D

It may be too much to expect that modern industry could perfectly achieve the purpose of providing soul-satisfying activity for every individual engaged in it, even if the initial placings and subsequent moves and promotions were handled in such a way as to take account as perfectly as possible of individual characteristics and abilities; but there can be no doubt that there is room for an enormous improvement of the present standards and conditions in these matters, and that this would go a long way toward achieving this purpose. It is one of the primary responsibilities of 'management' to concentrate attention on this and work for every possible improvement.

It is important to have a clear appreciation of what is involved. I must content myself with a compressed statement, and it is difficult to combine brevity with complete accuracy. But I would put the position something like this: The great majority of people are content to stay in the 'rank and file'. They do not seek responsibility for directing the work of others. This has its compensations, and I believe there is some truth in these words recently spoken by one of our leading industrialists,[11] who had himself started at the bottom:

Of one thing I am certain, and that is that to work with one's hands at a bench, at a machine, or, if you like, at a ledger, is much easier and more readily satisfying than work which involves a variety of decisions and the exercise of judgement. It is not so hard in the case of the former to feel that the job you were doing has been done, not only as well as you could do it, but as well as anybody could. It is not often that any member of top management can feel the same at the end of a day.

Of course, it is always easy to see attractions in the other fellow's job, and I cannot imagine that the speaker in this case would himself choose to go back to working at a bench; but nevertheless I believe that these words contain

[11] Sir Robert Sinclair, Chairman and Managing Director of Imperial Tobacco Co. Ltd. and President of the F.B.I., speaking at a British Institute of Management Conference, Harrogate, November 1950.

a substantial element of truth. What matters is, first, that the work for the majority who remain (and prefer to remain) in the ranks should be rightly handled and that they should have the opportunities of group comradeship and self-expression (to which I refer later); and, secondly, that there should be proper arrangements for identifying, and providing opportunities for, the minority who have the ambition and abilities for promotion. If the un-ambitious and ordinary majority have their work so arranged that they can enjoy group comradeship together, and if the ambitious minority are given the chance for full development of their faculties by promotion, then there are the makings of a community whose individual members can find happiness in their work.

All this points to the vital importance of providing well-devised arrangements for the selection and training of the minority who desire and deserve promotion. As to this, looking at the question from the point of view of the general body of workers, particular importance attaches to the arrangements for handling the first steps in promotion—that is to say, promotion to the grade of charge-hand, foreman, or supervisor, grades which may be called the N.C.Os. of industry. It is, of course, not only for those posts that good methods of selection and training are of importance; but a consideration of the methods used for filling these N.C.O. grades affords a good opportunity for making the points which are chiefly relevant to my present theme. I therefore take this case as an illustration.

I have before me as I write the draft of a report which has just been completed by the National Institute of Industrial Psychology, giving the results of a nation-wide survey in British industry of methods for the training, selection, and promotion of foremen and supervisors. This represents another of the series of research projects sponsored by the Panel on Human Factors to which I have already referred. This report (which involved visits

to a representative sample of over 100 firms and inter-
views with over 700 foremen) indicates that in a very
large proportion of British industry the methods employed
are still of a kind which can fairly be described as 'haphazard'.

Methods of Selection. Let me start with methods of
selection. Good methods should have a threefold object:
first, to find the best available man for every vacancy;
second, to make it clear to the whole body of workers that
a progressive career is open to merit and that promotion is
not dependent on luck or favouritism; and, third, to facili-
tate the giving of appropriate training and experience to
selected men before promotion.

Current methods of selection fall into two broad
categories. The first can be described as the method of
ad hoc nomination. The second relies on *systematic* selection
procedures which make use of such techniques as the
formal interviewing of candidates, the completion of
biographical history sheets, assessment on standardized
report or recommendation forms, intelligence or other
tests, the use of selection boards or panels, group selection
methods, and pre-promotional training-courses. The
methods of *ad hoc* nomination may work fairly well in
small concerns or in old family firms with a few hundred
employees, though there is always the danger that they
may be, or may appear to be, open to favouritism. But,
with the growing complexity of the foreman's job and
the growing size of industrial units, something more is
necessary, and it is clear that opinion in progressive firms
is moving toward recognizing the value of systematic
methods. It is notable, however, that of the firms examined in this survey, 72 per cent were judged to be
making their selections essentially on an *ad hoc* basis,
19 per cent had begun to introduce systematic methods
in more or less rudimentary form, and only 9 per cent
had well-developed systems.

Methods of Training. Next let me consider what is being done about *training* for the job. In the past, the general practice has been to rely on learning by trial and error, and by working under experienced supervisors. That must, of course, continue in the sense that there can be no substitute for experience. But picking up experience on the job is not alone enough. Formal and systematic training must be valuable, and the survey has shown clearly that this is the view of progressive firms and of the foremen themselves. Yet out of 721 foremen who were interviewed, only 40 per cent claimed to have had any training for their job—however little—while only 11 per cent had had more than elementary schooling.

I have chosen these two pieces of evidence on the selection and training of foremen merely as examples of the kind of matters which need attention if British industry is to do all that is possible to ensure that each individual is given the job for which he is best fitted and to feel that the way is open to him to make the best of his talents.

Some General Observations. Before I leave the subject heading of 'fitting the job to the man and the man to the job' I want to add some general observations, since it is in connexion with this subject that I can most appropriately expand my earlier short reference (p. 30) to the commonly expressed view that the conditions of modern industry, with its mass-production methods and the breakdown of skilled craftsman's jobs into repetitive, unskilled machine-minding operations, have made it impossible for the bulk of manual workers to find satisfying activity in their daily work. I want in the first place to register a protest against both the pessimism and the inaccuracy of this kind of sweeping generalization. Of course, there are problems here; but they should be faced with a determination to find solutions and not with a hopeless acquiescence in their insolubility. Then, when one comes to consider what the problems are, loose generalizations are misleading. There is a wide range of variety in modern industrial work. It is quite misleading to imagine that everybody is working on a conveyor belt. There is still a vast number of skilled jobs to be filled. Beyond this there is another important point to be noted. We must have our eyes, not on the past, but on the present and future. Conditions are constantly changing, and, looking ahead, there are possibilities of revolutionary developments. For example, the development of new electronic machines—calculating machines and machines for providing automatic control of repetitive operations may have a tremendous effect on human employment. Some acute observers foresee a second Industrial Revolution, with social consequences as important as the first.[12] If this kind of thing is to happen, there will, of course, be problems of social adjustment extending beyond the responsibilities of industrial managers; but it is for them to foresee and call attention to the problems and, looking at their responsibilities, the point which I want to emphasize is the need for constant active study of the possible reactions of new mechanical inventions. The questions ever present in their minds should be not merely what will be the economic effect of such inventions, but also—and this in my view is much the more important question—what effect such new developments will have on the lives of the workers for whose employment they are responsible.

I have referred to possibilities of the future because of the great need in this era of rapid technological development for constant adaptability. But there is already a vast

[12] This is the view, for example, of Dr. Norbert Wiener, Professor of Mathematics at the Massachusetts Institute of Technology. He foresees the displacement of large numbers of human workers and the need for opening up new fields of activity which will provide scope for the revival of local crafts and small specialized manufactures, etc. He has written on these subjects in his two books, one on *Cybernetics* and the other on *The Human Use of Human Beings*.

range of subjects which in existing conditions require attention, and of these I have given some illustrations.

My final word on the subject is this: Measures for 'fitting the job to the man and the man to the job' represent a main line of action for achieving the central purpose of making industrial work a satisfying activity. They must be supplemented by that other main line of action to which I have referred—namely, action to encourage the right kind of comradeship among working groups (pp. 38–9). It is these two lines of action, combined with the development of good systems of communication and joint consultation, that I regard as the chief positive measures for disproving the pessimistic view about the possibilities of modern industrial work.

Arrangements for the Division of the Proceeds of the Work

In my introductory paragraphs I made the point that the division of the proceeds was not the most important issue when one is considering how Christian principles should be applied, and I hope that in what I have said since then I have made clear my own views on the things which matter more. At the same time, it would be stupid and unrealistic to ignore the importance of all that is involved in the 'pay packet'. In order to get industrial work regarded in the way that I have been advocating, it is necessary that people should move away from the conception of industry as a conflict between two sides, and toward one of a co-operative effort for a common purpose; and this conception of a common purpose in the work has little chance of realization unless there is a general feeling that the system for the division of its proceeds is fair. I see this as a necessary condition precedent. No system of payment will take us all the way on the road to a true co-operative effort; but without a system which is, and is recognized as, fair, there is no chance of getting on to the road at all.

Now, there are two standards for judging pay, which for convenience I will distinguish as absolute and relative. Absolutely—is it *adequate* for the workers' needs? Relatively—is it *fair*: fair in relation to what other wage-earners are getting; fair in relation to the work done (effort, skill, discomfort, hazard, etc.); and, finally, fair in relation to profits and the total financial proceeds earned by the business? The 'absolute' standard is of course fundamentally important, since there can hardly be a satisfactory or harmonious industrial society unless everyone who is ready to do a fair day's work in industry can earn the means to satisfy what, according to current standards, are regarded as reasonable material needs. But the 'relative' standard is equally important and, indeed, in the conditions of today, I believe it is questions about this which require most consideration.

Let me therefore examine the three tests of fairness which I have stated above.

First, there is the question whether wages are fair in relation to what others are getting. As to this, all the evidence which I have seen goes to show that, once a certain minimum level of remuneration has been attained, it is questions of this kind which chiefly affect people's attitudes. Ideas that others are getting more for less, or less onerous, work, or that there are people who in one way or another are 'getting away with it', can be potent causes of dissatisfaction which operate against the impulse to go 'all out' in a true co-operative effort.

Next there is the question whether remuneration is fair in relation to the work done. This takes one into a field of difficult but vitally important issues. The introduction of pay systems which are, and can be accepted as, fairly related to the work-load carried and to the result produced can be a most powerful stimulus both to putting heart into the work and also to co-operation in the introduction of improved technical processes; and in this way not only can standards of remuneration be improved, but also the opportunities for satisfaction in work can be greatly increased. There is a tremendous task to be done here, since in large sections of British industry the systems for calculating the pay packet represent an almost unintelligible complex of patches and additions imposed on basic structures which were devised years ago in totally different conditions. (A good illustration of this is to be found in the recent reports of the Committee on the Wage System for Weavers in the Cotton Textile Industry.[13] This is an instructive case to study, since it shows, not only the nature of the problems and the need for improved systems, but also, unfortunately, the difficulty in getting such improved systems adopted even when unanimously recommended by a committee representing employers and trade unionists.) If there is to be any advance toward better pay-systems which are fairly related to the work-load, then there must be agreement between employers' and workers' representatives as to methods of work-measurement and job-appraisal. This is one of the matters in regard to which British industry has not progressed as far as American. For this relative backwardness I think both 'sides' share responsibility, but it is on the trade union side that the difference between this country and America is most marked. Some American trade unions employ their own very highly paid 'job-appraisal' technicians, so that the fixing of wage rates can be discussed as a matter to be agreed between experts rather than as a mere 'horse-trading' bargain between two opposing sides. There are welcome signs now of a considerable advance in opinion among the leading British trade unionists. I should like to express a hope that they will now take a lead in pressing for, and perhaps employing their own experts to participate in, research work aimed at making sure that the methods of work measurement,

[13] *Cotton Manufacturing Commission*, Parts I, II, III, and IV, 1948-9.

etc., are founded on a basis of scientific accuracy. If they do that, then they can be in advance of America.

Before I leave the subject of systems for settling rates of pay in relation to the work-load, I must mention another aspect of the matter which is of fundamental importance. To advocate such systems does not necessarily mean that one is advocating universal systems of piece-work rates. There is a tendency nowadays to suggest that the introduction of piece-work rates or 'incentive' methods of payment offers an easy way out of all difficulties. This is a dangerous over-simplification. I believe, indeed, that such methods, if carefully devised and introduced with general agreement, can be a great advance on systems now in use. But I do not believe they can provide the final solution. There are many dangers of abuse in the working of individual piece-work systems: scamped work, selfish rivalry, etc. To some extent, these may be got over by group bonus systems; but these, too, offer considerable difficulties. Moreover, there are large classes of work to which neither individual nor group bonus systems can be applied. My own view is that it may be necessary (at least in several industries) to go through a stage of trying out methods of this kind. They represent a step in evolution; and they can have an educative value. But I believe that for a final and satisfactory solution one must look forward to a state in which all can pull together and rely on appropriately graded rates of pay, fixed in relation to what has been settled by scientific methods of assessment to represent a fair day's work, and supported by a definite understanding that the rates will be progressively raised as results improve.

I am fully conscious that in making this statement I have left many complicating considerations undiscussed, but I hope its general significance will become clearer after I have examined the third test of 'fairness' to which I now turn—fairness in relation to profits earned, or to the total financial proceeds of the enterprise. Here we come to a key point. There are many who believe that, as long as there is any suspicion that private shareholders can get an unearned benefit from the results of better effort by the workers, the latter will not put their hearts into the work and will withhold full co-operation from measures designed to improve production. It is this belief, of course, which has provided one of the main arguments for nationalization. In this belief, too, there are a few privately owned firms that have accepted a self-denying ordinance for restricting dividends to a moderate fixed percentage, leaving the disposal of any surplus to be decided by a works council on which the workers are represented. And, finally, this same belief has found less drastic expression in profit-sharing schemes.

One can argue at great length for and against measures of this kind, and a number of complex issues are involved. I must content myself with a brief statement of my own views, based on much discussion and reflection. I believe that none of these methods meets the real needs. It may be too early to assess the full effects of the nationalization schemes which have already been introduced. (And in any case, if one is to be fair, one ought to judge their effects in relation to what would have been the position if they had not been introduced.) Nevertheless, it is surely clear that the mere fact that such profits as are earned must now go to the State and not to private shareholders has failed to eliminate disputes about wages or to create an all-out co-operative effort to improve production. As to the device of dividend limitation, I believe that this, too, is by itself inadequate, and, further, that it involves a rigidity which is not suitable to the system on which the great bulk of British industry still has to be conducted. It remains to consider profit-sharing schemes. Such schemes may, and indeed have, produced useful results in the case of certain undertakings which operate in conditions of considerable stability. But even in these exceptional cases profit-sharing does not provide a full solution of the fundamental problem, while for the general run of industry I think it can make very little contribution at all. The main reason is that profits are affected by so many factors which cannot in any way be influenced by the workers. The results of a first-class production effort can, so far as profits are concerned, be completely offset by errors in commercial policy (bad buying, bad judgement of markets, bad salesmanship, etc.) or by changes in world conditions. Even so far as the production side is concerned, the workers' efforts may be neutralized by bad production planning, mistaken design of products, etc. Further, if an element of a share in profits comes to be relied on as an addition to basic wages, and if then it disappears owing to no fault of the workers, that must lead to dissatisfaction.

What, then, is required? My own belief is that the vital points are, first, to give the workers complete (and, I emphasize, complete) information about financial as well as technical results, and, secondly, to have it accepted as a binding principle that, as financial results improve, basic pay rates will be raised. On the basis of full information and this binding principle, the aim must be to satisfy the workers, first, that they are getting what the industry can afford to pay, and, secondly, that what the industry 'can afford to pay' is not limited by avoidable incompetence.

I believe that this statement gives an idea of the correct formula, and that it applies just as much to nationalized industries as to private enterprise. At the same time, I certainly do not claim that I have provided an easy solution. My formula is generalized and complex. The precise application of its various elements involves many difficulties. Thus, there are obviously difficult questions to be answered before assessing what an enterprise can 'afford to pay'. (For example, what is the proper return on capital, taking into account not only the obligation to be fair to those who have in the past provided the capital but also what is needed to attract such additional capital in the future as may be required if the enterprise is to keep its place in progress? Or again, how far should the benefits of reduced costs of production be passed on to consumers in lower prices rather than to workers in increased wages?) Yet I believe that the real difficulties will be limited to two key problems. The first is the problem of communication—of getting the full information across to the workers so that there may be a true understanding of the position. The second is the problem which arises out of my phrase, 'that what the industry can afford to pay is not limited by avoidable incompetence'. If these two problems can be solved, I do not fear that the workers' side will be unreasonable in agreeing to what is a fair distribution and in recognizing the claims other than their own which have to be taken into account.

Of the two 'key problems', the first, that of 'communication', will be the subject of my next main heading. It is with the second, therefore, that I wish to deal at this stage. This problem of satisfying the workers' side that 'what the industry can afford to pay is not limited by avoidable incompetence' is one of great practical significance. Looking back over the past history of British industry, there can be no doubt (as, indeed, I have already commented) that the excuse, 'We cannot afford to pay more', has often been used as a protective cover for inefficiency and that maintenance of profit margins or the avoidance of losses has been sought by cutting wages when it ought (not only on Christian principles, but also in the national interest) to have been found by increasing technical efficiency.[14]

[14] If anyone questions this, let him examine the way in which the Lancashire cotton textile industry tackled its problems in the inter-war years (when there was a superfluity of labour) and contrast that with the search for increased efficiency today (when labour is in short supply).

What has happened in the past, unfortunately, but inevitably, influences the attitude on the workers' side today. If this influence of past memories is allowed to survive, and if British industry is to continue working on the basis of 'two sides' pulling against each other, then the normal trade union attitude is likely to remain the negative one of saying: 'It is not our responsibility to study production efficiency or to show how, or by how much, an industry can afford to increase its rates of pay by technical improvements. That is the employers' responsibility. Our only course is to go on pressing for increased wages and thus force the employers to improve their methods and equipment for production.'

My own profound conviction is that such an attitude is out of date and wrong. If it were to continue to determine policy on the workers' side, then there could be little hope either of achieving the material success necessary for national survival or of creating conditions in which men can put their hearts into their work and thus get true satisfaction from it.

But, fortunately, there are clear signs that British trade union leaders are now adopting a different conception of their role and are seeking ways by which they can take their share as partners in a constructive effort to improve methods of production as the only sure way forward, whether the objective is seen as national survival or the improvement of the lot of their members. Yet there is much to be done before this conception can be translated into effective action along the whole labour front.

This is a matter of great importance, and since I believe that a comparison between the practices of British and American trade unions helps to throw light on it, I want to say something on this.

It is, I believe, broadly true to say that the American unions have concentrated on advancing the conditions for the best workers (accepting high standards for a good day's work and not worrying about the weaker brethren who fail to make the grade), whereas the British unions have endeavoured rather to establish minimum standards for each industry as a whole, below which none shall fall. Consistently with this idea, it has been characteristic of the American unions to support wage agreements for individual firms; to get the most favourable rates possible accepted by the most efficient firms and then to put pressure on the less efficient to come into line; and finally (at least this has happened in certain cases), to say to the inefficient firms who claim that they cannot afford to pay these rates: 'We will send our own experts along to over-haul your organization and methods so as to show you how you can get into a position where you *can* afford it.' Several American unions, as I have already mentioned, employ highly paid experts so that they can give advice in special cases of this kind and talk as equals with the experts on the management side when matters of work measurement, job-appraisal, and rate-fixing have to be discussed. I am very far from suggesting that the British trade unions should copy the Americans in every respect, and I certainly do not want to see them abandon their more human outlook; but on this particular matter I am con-vinced that the time has come when they should move nearer to the American practice. And, indeed, it is clear from several recent publications that many leading British trade unionists are thinking on these lines. If they do this, they can make a most important contribution to the solution of the particular problem which I have been discussing, and thus aid a move forward along the one road which opens out a hopeful line of progress.

Summary of Discussion on Division of Proceeds of Work

I must now pull together the threads of thought that I have been following out on the matter of pay or division of the proceeds. What I have been trying to say is this: I do not believe that any set patterns for schemes of dividend limitation or profit-sharing will by themselves provide the right way for satisfying the workers that they are getting a fair return, so clearly as to destroy all the suspicions and inhibitions which tend to hold them back from going 'all out' and putting their hearts into their work in a joint co-operative effort. Nor do I believe that nationalization, as a means of securing that profits go to the State rather than to private shareholders, will achieve that result. The objective to be aimed at is a form of community co-operation (within each factory, but backed by the trade unions) in which all ranks can feel that they have an interest in improving production results and an opportunity to contribute to such improvement and can satisfy themselves that the proceeds are fairly divided. The most satisfactory form of fair division is to be achieved not by systems which make individuals compete with each other (incentive piece-work rates, etc.), but by basic wage rates which are founded on an accurate assessment of a fair day's work, and which are steadily advanced as production results improve. British industry as a whole is still a very long way from achieving this kind of community co-operation (though some hopeful experiments are already going on in particular firms). It can only be achieved on a foundation of enlightened opinion from the floor upwards and full understanding by the workers of the policy and results of their firm; and this is necessary, not only as a means to better results, but also as a condition in which each can get greater satisfaction from his work. How to create this condition of enlightened opinion and full understanding is the subject of my next heading, to which I now turn.

Methods of Communication and Joint Consultation

The preceding paragraphs have pointed to two needs: first, the need to communicate information to the workers in a way which will enable them to understand the firm's production and financial policy together with the working results of such policy and all the external conditions which affect such results; secondly, the need to consult the workers through their representatives before decisions of policy are taken or before working arrangements are settled. No mere one-way communication of unilateral authoritarian decisions can be effective to create the kind of community co-operation which I have postulated as an objective.

So far as concerns methods of *communication*, this is a subject on which further study is particularly necessary. I believe that quite an important part of any industrial trouble that we have today is caused by the failure of one side to understand correctly what the other side has tried to say. I believe there is great room for improvement in the technique of 'getting things across', and that all who carry managerial responsibilities should interest themselves in getting research done in this field. (One of the projects of the Panel on Human Factors to which I have referred is a study of methods of communication.)

I pass from this to *joint consultation*, which, of course, in itself is partly valuable as an instrument of communication. This is a part of my subject which alone requires a whole volume for adequate treatment. I can only touch on a few key points. It is very important for my main theme, because here one comes to arrangements the effectiveness of which depends entirely on the spirit in which they are worked. That spirit must be essentially Christian, having regard to each individual as a human being. Without that, no formal arrangements can be more than 'sounding brass or a tinkling cymbal'. Proper arrangements for 'joint consultation' must be both formal (in committees, etc.) and informal (in all daily contacts). They must be introduced with a clearly envisaged purpose. It is useless to regard joint consultation as a kind of remedy for industrial troubles which can be made up

E

according to a standardized prescription. On the contrary, the arrangements must be adjusted to the conditions in each case and must be designed for specific objects. The broad aim must be to create a community with a common purpose; and this must be seen as having value in two ways: first, for the good of the individual workers; second, for the sake of effective production results. For the individual worker, methods of joint consultation can help to bring about many of the results which I have already mentioned. They can help him to understand the purpose and policy of the firm and the place of his own job in it; to feel that he counts as a person, that he has a part to play the importance of which is recognized, and that his work is appreciated; to feel that he has some freedom for self-expression in his work, in the sense that he has a chance to have a say about how his own daily job is handled; to give a foundation for confidence in his leaders by creating an understanding of why things are done in a certain way; and, finally, to give him the chance to satisfy himself that the proceeds of the firm's work are fairly divided. In all these ways he can be helped to feel that he can put his heart into his work and thus to get satisfaction from it.

As to the second purpose—the purpose of helping the effective working of the firm—the chief value of joint consultative methods is as an aid to the kind of decentralization to which I have referred under the heading of organization: the state of affairs in which every decision is taken at the level where it can most effectively be taken. Here one comes to a difficult aspect of the matter, involving questions of leadership, discipline, etc. Joint consultation is usually, and quite rightly seen as a method for bringing about a sharing of responsibility. The difficulty is to have a sharing of responsibility without getting responsibilities confused or divided. I think this difficulty can be overcome, but there is need for clear thinking on this matter. The chief executive officer in an industrial undertaking, like a military commander, has certain responsibilities for leadership and decision which it is wrong for him to unload on to others. But that does not mean that he should not help all ranks to understand the reasons for his decisions, or that he should not try to get ideas from consultation with them before he takes his decisions or settles his general plan of action. Further, it does not mean that the top executive or military commander must himself take *every* decision. In the conduct of any industrial enterprise, just as in a military operation, there are different levels at which decisions can be taken. There is a 'right' level for the decision in each particular case, and, as I have already remarked, the essence of good organization is to ensure that each decision shall be taken at the level where it can be most rapidly and effectively taken. The way, therefore, must be opened for 'decentralized' decisions, and the point which I want to make now is that decentralized decisions cannot be well taken unless they are based on sufficient understanding of the central purpose. This indicates one of the most valuable aims of joint consultative methods—to spread among all ranks knowledge and understanding of the central purpose of an industrial firm's policy. Much has been said and written in recent years about the way in which this idea of keeping all ranks informed of the central purpose was applied in military operations of the last war. Montgomery's methods with the Eighth Army are always regarded as an outstanding example. But our best commanders have had these ideas before, and it is recorded that Nelson once said that his ideal pattern was 'individual freedom within an *understood* framework of discipline and order'. That is a good phrase.

It is easy to appreciate the value of the two broad purposes which I have outlined; but it would be a great mistake to suppose that it is easy to devise practical arrangements which provide a fully adequate instrument for achieving them. A considerable body of experience on this matter now exists in British industry, since various types of joint consultation procedure have now been practised in numerous firms for several years. Here is a subject in relation to which I want to refer back to what I have already said about the obligations of those managing our industrial firms to observe, interpret, and make known the results of their own experience. Several firms have done this, and much has been written on the subject; but there is a need for more systematic record and evaluation of developing experiences.

On this matter I hope that a valuable contribution to knowledge will be made by two of the research projects sponsored by the Panel on Human Factors affecting Productivity, to which I have already at several points referred. The first of these is a nation-wide survey (conducted by the National Institute of Industrial Psychology) of how joint consultative procedure is actually working today in British industry. The second is an intensive study of an experiment in 'industrial democracy' made by a successful company in the engineering industry employing about 1,500 people.[15] This company has been for some years attempting to work out a very real and complete system for giving all ranks a chance to share responsibility in settling policy (including financial policy) as well as in arranging the daily conduct of its operations. A team of research workers from the Tavistock Institute has been collaborating in working through these developments and in maintaining a full day-to-day 'case history' record, following out the evolution of various different types of arrangement, the reactions which they have set up, and the way in which human attitudes have revealed themselves. I cannot attempt to deal fully with the results of these two research projects, since, at the time of my own

[15] The Glacier Metal Company.

writing, the reports on them have not yet been completed. It is sufficient for my present purpose to indicate some broad conclusions.

These are that methods of joint consultation must be kept fluid and ready for constant evolutionary change, since what is demanded and what is practicable will be constantly changing as the general level of education is raised and as experience is gained in working together. Further, no method can be fully or permanently successful unless the 'management side' (a) wholeheartedly believe in the process and want it to be successful; (b) are ready to give the 'workers' side' full information on all that affects the operation of their business; (c) are ready to take real account of the views expressed by the workers' side before introducing new methods which affect the daily handling of their jobs as well as before deciding policy; (d) are ready to strive for the ultimate success of the arrangements with great patience and determination in spite of disappointments and difficulties which might not unreasonably be used as an excuse for abandoning the whole attempt.

The last words are important. As I have already said, joint consultation is a two-way business, and its success cannot be secured by any mere unilateral effort on the part of management. There must be an adequate response on the workers' side, and an examination of what has been actually happening in this matter makes it clear that it would be quite unrealistic to assume that the 'workers' in general are immediately ready to take a keen, intelligent interest, and are merely waiting for an opportunity to respond. A good deal of what is being done today under the title of joint consultation is of petty significance—useful perhaps as an opportunity for ventilating grievances, but poles apart from that full community collaboration which I have postulated. On the other hand, those firms which are genuinely working toward this objective are encountering real difficulties.

The greatest of these difficulties is apparent apathy. If a full measure of joint consultation is genuinely tried, then committee meetings take up much time and involve a very real sacrifice for those who serve as committee members. If their constituents take little interest in their efforts, that is not only discouraging for them, but also makes their task of 'reporting back' extremely difficult, with the result that the general body of workers remain uninformed. Such evidence as I have seen suggests that there tends to be a live interest in committee meetings when some subject of acute concern to the rank and file is in the air (for example, the handling of a 'redundancy' problem such as occurred in many factories during the latter half of 1949 before devaluation); but that in ordinary times there is considerable apathy.

Another difficulty is that useful discussion in joint consultation, especially when such matters as financial policy have to be considered, requires a higher level of intelligence and education than is at present always available.

Then again, the workers' representatives are by no means always ready to welcome the chance of sharing in the responsibility for decisions. A not uncommon reaction is that management is trying to unload its own proper responsibilities on to the workers' shoulders.

Finally, I must mention a difficulty of a different kind. If a firm is trying, through methods of joint consultation and otherwise, to weld all its ranks into a co-operating community, the question arises whether the internal loyalties thus created may be in conflict with the workers' loyalty to their trade unions. This is a question which must be faced and to which I shall return again.

I believe all these difficulties can be overcome,[16] and I

---

[16] As regards the difficulties within the firm, it is perhaps fair to comment that it would be remarkable if such difficulties were not encountered. The fact is that to devise democratic methods which give scope for individual self-expression and a sharing of responsibility, while at the same time maintaining central guiding direction, is an intrinsically difficult problem.

have mentioned them at this stage because, in considering the responsibilities of management, it is so essential to recognize the need for patience, sympathy and flexibility expressed in a readiness to learn by experience, and to work out a line of progress by trial and careful observation of different types of arrangements. In a later passage I shall attempt to give a fuller appreciation of the true significance of the difficulties, and to discuss the means for overcoming them; but at this point, having dealt with all the five subject headings which I mentioned at the beginning of this series (p. 37), I can conveniently consider where I have got in the development of my line of thought.

A Review of the Discussion up to this Point

In my introductory paragraphs (p. 17) I said that there were three elements of human relations to be considered: first, the behaviour of 'management' to 'workers'; second, the response of the workers (their attitude to management and their work); and, third, the relations of the workers with each other (the association and co-operation of the individual with his fellow workers, which includes the important matter of relations with trade unions). Up to this point I have been focusing attention on the first element, and have approached every subject from the side of the representatives of management; but, in considering joint consultation, I have been led into a discussion of the workers' response, while, both here and also at several other points, I have mentioned questions affecting relations with the trade unions. In order to give balance to my review, I must now turn to a more general consideration of these second and third 'elements'.

The same kind of intrinsic difficulty is becoming apparent now in the development of Parliamentary procedure, especially in relation to the new responsibilities falling on Government as a result of its greater intervention in economic life or of the nationalization of certain industries. It is not only in industry, therefore, but in every sphere of life and at every level that there is a need to evolve new techniques of democratic procedure. This must be a long process carried out largely by trial and error.

THREE

THE SECOND ASPECT OF HUMAN RELATIONS IN INDUSTRY—THE WORKERS' RESPONSE

IT WOULD, of course, be absurd to suggest that the responsibilities rest only on the side of management. Management must indeed take the lead in the measures which I have discussed; but, if there is to be any hope of creating a Christian industrial society, Christian principles must be a guide for the conduct of all ranks. No measures that management can take to create conditions for making work a happy activity can fulfil that purpose unless the workers on their side have the right attitude to work (which, according to the views which I have expressed, means that they must see the earning of their daily bread as a condition of self-respect, and recognize that good work well done can be an end in itself and the foundation of a happy life). Again, no attempts by management to create a genuine co-operating community in each factory can succeed unless there is a readiness among all ranks to pull together. And, finally, of course, it must be recognized that we shall fail as a nation in the mere earning of our daily bread (as that is now interpreted) unless there is some measure of success along the lines that I have indicated.

I feel it necessary at this point to insert one more elementary statement of my own interpretation of Christian principles. There is always a danger that to advocate a progressive and generous policy for management, such as I have described, may be taken to imply softness and sentimentality. But there is nothing soft or sentimental in Christian principles. What the Sermon on the Mount condemns is personal rancour as between one man and another, not anger at what is wrong or fighting against it. Christ did not seek appeasement with the money-lenders in the Temple. He threw them out. Nor did He ever say anything against the idea of discipline or the exercise of leadership and command when that is necessary for the conduct of an enterprise in which many have to be engaged together. St. Paul, too, was speaking as a Christian and using words which equally need saying today when he wrote to the Thessalonians:

For even when we were with you, this we commanded you, that if any would not work, neither should he eat. For we hear that there are some which walk among you disorderly, working not at all, but are busy-bodies (2 Thessalonians 3[10-11]).

It is right, therefore, to say that there must be a proper response on the workers' side, and what I want now to consider is what are the influences affecting this response and in what form it should express itself.

The General Conditions affecting Workers' Attitudes

A Transition Period. There are today a number of particular influences at work; but overriding all there is a general condition which must be understood. As I see it, we stand at the beginning of a social revolution characterized by new attitudes and expectations on the workers' side and a strong reaction against the old status of the dependent wage-earner. Many causes have been and are at work: the cumulative effect of extended education, the break in old traditions brought about largely by two world wars, the more effective power of 'labour' in politics, the strengthened economic position of 'labour' resulting from full employment conditions, and a number more. The full force of these influences is only just beginning, and the transition stage in which we now stand is an awkward one. The workers are groping for something new to replace the old authoritarian system; but they have no clear conception of the pattern for a new system to take its place, nor are they yet able or ready fully to provide the skills and undertake the responsibilities which a more 'democratic' system would require. The one thing which is clear is that nationalization has failed to provide the new system and status which they want.

I recognize that to many this may seem an exaggerated and over-dramatized appreciation of the present position, and it is, of course, true that much of the impetus of old habits and traditions is still continuing and keeping many activities going. But this impetus must eventually run down, and the urgent need is to have some new pattern of human relations built into our industrial system before that happens. It may well be that those firms which are taking the boldest steps in developing methods of joint consultation and industrial democracy are, at the moment, in advance of their time; but if there is to be any progress there must always be some reformers who are in advance of their time, and in this case my belief is that the lines on which such firms are trying to find ways forward are the lines of true progress, that there is the greatest value in their pioneering efforts, and that it would be fatal to be discouraged by the difficulties which they may now be meeting.

But, whether these particular efforts are rightly directed or not, I am convinced that, in order to understand the present position, we must realize that we do now stand in an awkward period of transition, that this has got to be worked through, and that, until a new basis has been established which is in harmony with the workers' expectations (a basis of willing co-operation), there will inevitably be symptoms of malaise and maladjustment. I think this general condition is having a wide influence and explains much of what may be unsatisfactory in workers' attitudes today. At the same time, I do not believe that our general condition is diseased or decadent. In spite of many disturbing symptoms, there is plenty of evidence to show that, where management has been functionally efficient and where human relations have been well handled, the workers have responded in a way which encourages hopes for further progress. There is a certain percentage of workers (as indeed there always will be) who, in St. Paul's words, 'walk disorderly, working not at all, but are busy-bodies'. But, so far as the great bulk of workers are concerned, I believe that the right attitudes to work and co-operation are there, and can be evoked into adequate expression in action, provided that certain obstructive influences can be removed and certain potentially disturbing influences rightly handled.

Obstructive Influences. I want now briefly to examine some of these influences.

Among obstructive influences the greatest of all is suspicion. As I have already said, 'the whole industrial field is bedevilled with suspicions based on past memories. As a result, even the most honest attempts to improve human relations tend to be viewed with mistrust—either as dodges to get something extra out of the workers for the benefit of the profit-makers or as signs of a temporary mood "produced by force of circumstances rather than a change of heart".' The only way to overcome these suspicions is for management to pursue with complete honesty the kind of purposes which I have indicated and to develop methods of communication and joint consultation in such a way that the purposes are really understood.

Next there are the commonly alleged difficulties resulting from the conditions of modern industry. Here I am brought back once more to questions on which I have already touched at several points.[1] Is it true that

[1] See pp. 30 and 53.

the increasing size of industrial undertakings has so destroyed all chance of close human relationships between management and workers as to make it vain to advocate the kind of human co-operative effort which I have set out as the right aim? Is it true that the methods of mass production have so destroyed all chance of the joy in craftsmanship for the great bulk of workers as to make it unrealistic to expect what I have described as the right attitude to work among manual workers? I have taken the line that both these questions point to real difficulties which demand the best efforts to overcome them, but that the sweeping generalizations which they imply are quite unwarranted. The size of a large concern need not make its management impersonal and inhuman, provided that the organization is such as to allow a proper measure of decentralization which, to quote my own earlier words, will ensure that 'each decision is taken at the level at which it can best be taken'. Some of the largest of the British industrial combines are tackling this problem and are in the forefront of progress in the proper handling of human relations. It is the nationalized industries which today are chiefly at fault in this respect (though among them too there are great variations—for example, as between the nationalized gas industry with its decentralized 'federal' structure and the Coal Board with its centralized unitary organization). As to the loss of the 'craftsman' interest, the view which I have expressed has been that if all possible steps are taken (on the lines which I have indicated) for 'fitting the job to the man and the man to the job', for organizing the workers in working groups of the right size, and for information and joint consultation, the disadvantages of modern mass production methods can be largely overcome. In a sense it is true to say that the craftsman's job in certain cases has been transferred from the individual to the group. As I said in my opening paragraph, the adjustment of men to highly mechanized work by its very nature requires a high degree of co-operation. If harmonious working groups can be created, then there can be the important complementary advantage of working together as members of a team instead of in isolation. If there are difficulties today in human attitudes to work, I believe that these are mainly due to the deeper-seated conditions of what I have described as the present 'transition period' rather than to the large size of firms or methods of mass production. (Otherwise, just to take one illustration, there would, in the matter of attitudes to work, be a marked difference between workers in large factories and workers on farms, where there is still close personal contact between all ranks and where the importance of craftsmanship has, if anything, been increased by modern methods. This certainly is not the case. Indeed, if there is any difference it seems fair to say that morale and attitudes to work are better in manufacturing industry than among agricultural workers.)

The Conditions of Full Employment. I have next to consider a different kind of factor—the condition of full employment. Here indeed is a factor which has been a special characteristic of the post-war years and which has important and complex influences. First, one must take account of the belief (and there are many who hold this belief in their hearts—far more than openly express it) that, human nature being what it is, a full work effort will not be forthcoming without the drive of necessity, the spur of fear—fear of losing one's job and of resulting poverty. It is no use meeting this belief with a flat denial. If one is to be realistic, one must admit that it contains an element of truth—that it may be partially true of many people and wholly true of a few. The real question is what action should be taken on it. No one dares to argue that we should deliberately endeavour to re-create the large-scale unemployment of the inter-war years; but there are quite a number of people who want to be 'realistic' but at the same time 'progressive', and who take the line that it would be healthy to bring about a moderate measure of unemployment—just enough to give people a touch of the stick, a whiff of necessity. Now, I don't believe that things can be so nicely regulated, and I don't believe one can have it both ways. I think we have got to make the choice and ask ourselves these questions: Do we believe in going back to the old system or forward to something new? Shall we put our trust in evoking willing co-operation or do we want to rely on forcing people to work by the discipline of fear? Do we believe in playing down to the worst elements in human nature or playing up to the best? Here indeed is a clear case for the application of Christian principles. The Christian, surely, must believe in playing up to the best. That is one of the most vital elements in love as St. Paul has described it in the First Epistle to the Corinthians. But—and this is the essential point in all that I have to say—it is not enough merely to take this as a kind-hearted and trustful choice. We must use our minds for working out practical arrangements—arrangements for evoking the best elements, for removing the obstacles to their exercise, and for giving them full scope. And we must have the patience and faith to continue these efforts in the face of inevitable disappointments. Those who stand for this choice can justify themselves by the lessons of past history. Looking back over this, we can find many occasions when there has been conflict over the same sort of choice between 'playing up to the best or down to the worst'. As I have been writing these words, I have been reading the latest life of Florence Nightingale. How astounding it is today to read the arguments of the 'realists' at the time of the Crimea who believed that to introduce humane methods for treating the wounded would destroy the necessary toughness of the British soldiers. Florence Nightingale, by her life's work, answered such arguments. They cropped up indeed at many points in her campaign for Army reforms, and she was always ready to fight them with action and argument and humour.

It has [she wrote] been said by officers enthusiastic in their profession that there are three causes which make a soldier enlist, namely, being out of work, in a state of intoxication, or jilted by his sweetheart. Yet the incentives to enlistment which we desire to multiply could hardly be put by Englishmen of the nineteenth century in this form, namely, more poverty, more drink, more faithless sweethearts.

So equally today I am convinced that it must be both futile and wrong to seek to increase the stimulus to work by increasing the fear of unemployment. We must find a better way. There is, moreover, another very important aspect of this question which reinforces this view. There are, in fact, the strongest positive and practical reasons for endeavouring to maintain conditions of full employment. Our national survival today depends on increasing productivity, and for this it is essential that all restrictive practices in industry should be abandoned and that the ranks of labour should co-operate with management in the introduction of every possible 'labour-saving' arrangement (better equipment, better deployment of the labour force, etc.). There have in the past been formidable resistances to this kind of development, and these have by no means yet entirely disappeared. Most of these resistances can, in one way or another, be traced back to fears of unemployment—fears that, by working better, men may work themselves out of a job. If it is possible now to eliminate these fears by creating a real faith in the continuance of full employment, then there can be a new hope for a fundamental change of attitude on the workers' side and for the adoption by the trade unions of that new conception of their role for which I have pleaded—a conception of constructive partnership with management in improving the processes of production. I can think of

nothing in the field of practical considerations which is
more important than this.

External Influences

Education. Up to the present I have been considering the
influence of conditions within the industrial field; but
influences from outside have also to be considered, and
today many of these are at work. A fundamentally
important influence of this kind is that of education. Here
I must exercise self-restraint. To mention education takes
me to the threshold of a vast and intensely interesting
field. I am tempted to discuss many aspects, but for my
present purpose I am concerned essentially with one
question: What is going to be the effect of education as
now given (and of the educational opportunities which
have now been opened) on people's attitudes to manual
work and on their chance of finding scope for self-realization and satisfaction in such work?

I speak as one who has always stood for educational
expansion and who in the House of Commons strongly
supported the Act of 1944. But, at the same time, I believe
that there is urgent need for studying how the new policy
is working out and for being ready to adapt it according
to its results. We are committed now to a policy of an
educated nation with equality of opportunity for all.
(Though the full realization will take time, we crossed
the Rubicon with the 1944 Act.) Have all the implications of this been provided for? Can we be satisfied that
we have devised the right forms of universal secondary
education so far as concerns the vast majority who will
pass out of full-time school education at the statutory
leaving age and who will have to spend their lives in some
form of manual labour? How will their short period of
school education leave them adapted for their lives? Will
it be something which, while valuable for the minority
as the first stage of a longer course of school and

University education, is also for the vast majority a satisfactory whole in itself? Or will it be just a truncated period which leaves them in the air? Will it provide a basic foundation which will give them a right scale of values and a guide to their way through life? And what in particular will be its effect on attitudes to *manual* work? We have now accepted (and in my view rightly accepted) a classless conception of equality of opportunity in education; but have we, as a nation, yet acquired a classless conception of society itself or of the implications of education? Are we not still carrying forward the idea that the educated individual must get out of manual work and that it constitutes 'social advance' to do so? If so, is not education going to be an influence tending to create internal conflict, unhappiness, and a wrong attitude to work among the great numbers who will inevitably have to spend their lives in manual tasks? How can that danger be countered?

Questions like these have got to be faced. In stating them, I by no means imply a belief that they cannot be answered, and I certainly do not imply regret that the great forward moves in educational policy have been taken. What I do assert is that there is an urgent need to study how our educational policy is working out and what reactions it is setting up. In particular, I want to stress the importance of ensuring that education is so handled as to help people to get full value from their *work*, whatever form that work may take. I want to protest against the conception of education as a process which does no more than prepare the soul for the enjoyment of leisure when practical needs have been satisfied. It should be a preparation for getting the best self-realization out of all life's activities. We can have no healthy industrial society if our system of education is one which makes those whom it influences able to find happiness only in escape from their breadwinning work.

F

These questions, of course, raise issues which extend far beyond the responsibilities of industrial leaders as such. But I believe that industrial leaders can make a valuable contribution, and should give this a high place among their responsibilities. As an aid to finding proper answers, I believe it is important to have close contact and collaboration between the world of education and the world of industry. Industrialists (and here I include trade unionists as well as 'management') should interest themselves in the study of how our educational system is working. Beyond this, industrial employers have themselves a definite educational responsibility. And that means much more than giving facilities for part-time education to their young employees. It means handling the work of the young entrants in an educational way; it means ensuring that all those responsible for supervising this work, and especially foremen, are capable of doing this; it means watching all employees to discover talent; it means telling the educational world what industry wants; it means ability to value and make the best use of what that world can give.

If all these points are fully studied, then education can be a powerful instrument for aiding the nation's progress and for giving fuller and happier lives to its individual members. But thorough study by all concerned (especially industrialists) is needed. Mere benevolent support for the idea of expanding education is not enough.

Other External Influences. There are today many other external influences which can affect attitudes to work and 'the workers' reponse'. I must content myself with a brief mention of two more, which I select as helping to bring out the points which I think chiefly need attention.

Social Security Benefits. First there is the possible effect of our social security policy. A question which is causing some concern today is whether the provision of high sickness benefits is likely to produce a serious and unjustifiable increase in sickness absence. Evidence and opinions on the question are conflicting. My own conclusion from such evidence as I have seen is that what happens in this matter is a good index of industrial morale. In firms where human relations have been well handled and where industrial morale is good, the provision of high rates of sickness benefit has not been followed by an increase in the rate of sickness absence—indeed, rather the reverse. Where there has been an increase, this is *prima facie* evidence that there is room for improvement in industrial morale (though that may be a condition due to tradition in an industry as a whole rather than to the conduct of individual firms). I recognize that this is a provocative conclusion, and I would include this as one of the questions which requires further study.

Compulsory National Service. The other external influence which I want to mention is that of compulsory National Service on the young industrial entrant. Obviously, the two years' interruption at an impressionable age can have a powerful influence on outlook and character. I want to urge that National Service should be regarded not as a necessary evil, but as a tremendous opportunity for exerting a valuable influence on character and general education. And toward taking advantage of this opportunity industrial leaders can greatly help. Much can be done by seeing that the period of employment before the call-up is treated as an educational period, and thereby giving to all the young employees (and not merely those who enter an indentured apprenticeship justifying deferment) a feeling that they have got a foundation on which to build and to which they can return. Much, too, can be done by helping them before they are called up to get a practical understanding of what life in the Forces will mean. Here is a case where there is a marked difference between the practice of different employers. I could quote several examples of firms which have developed most admirable schemes of educational preparation for the call-up, and in fact have done everything possible (and I believe with great chances of success) to ensure that National Service is a positive influence for good and not a disturbing or demoralizing influence or a mere waste of time.

The Need for Continuous Study of all these Influences

I have considered a number of influences which can affect attitudes to work and workers' response: the nature of modern industrial methods, conditions of full employment, education, high sickness benefits, compulsory National Service. They all have the common feature that their effects need constant objective study, that they can be powerful influences for good or bad according to the way in which they are handled, and that industrial leaders can play a big part both in their study and in their handling and should regard it as part of their duty as Christians to recognize this as an essential element of their responsibility.

Summary of Views as to the Workers' Response

It is, however, as influences affecting the 'workers' response' that I have been considering these questions, and I must now briefly sum up the general significance of all the influences and considerations that I have discussed.[2]

According to the philosophy of life and the interpretation of Christian principles which I have tried to state, the undertaking of creative work in a spirit of service is an essential condition for a good life on this earth.

The provision of the material conditions for such a life can only be made secure, or worth securing, if all members

---

[2] In this and the next paragraphs, I follow closely the wording of a passage in a report of a conference of theologians, business men, trade unionists, and economists, called by the late Archbishop Temple (*Man's Work and the Christian Faith*, published in 1948 by the Industrial Christian Fellowship). The passage is one for which I had the main drafting responsibility.

of the community recognize their responsibilities to the community.

Good material conditions can only fulfil their proper purpose, or be saved from becoming a positively demoralizing influence, if the moral state of the individual is such that he does not overvalue these things, and this means that his release from preoccupation with his own material cares is to be taken, not as an occasion for slackening in his work or in his service to the community, but as an opportunity for developing his own highest qualities.

To Christians, service to the community implies consideration of the needs of others in a spirit of love, and that not only gives the surest basis for service, but ennobles every act.

I have expressed the belief that, provided that certain causes of suspicion and friction can be removed and certain external influences rightly handled, there is reason to hope that the right kind of response will be forthcoming from the general body of workers, and that a choice to go forward in this hope is the only possible course for those who believe in Christian principles.

FOUR

THE THIRD ASPECT OF HUMAN RELATIONS IN INDUSTRY—THE RELATION OF THE WORKERS WITH EACH OTHER

IN ALL that I have been saying, I have emphasized the fundamental need for treating each worker as a human personality whose individual expression and development must be regarded as of supreme value. But it is equally necessary to recognize that the individual cannot have any full development or self-expression except as a member of a community. This has a special significance in industrial employment. In considering the individual's association and co-operation with his fellow workers, it is not enough merely to state one's belief that the only sure foundation for the right kind of association is the religious conception of Christian brotherhood. That is indeed my belief, but it is also necessary to examine by what practical means, in the conditions of modern industry, men can best give expression to the ideal of brotherhood as between fellow workers. Here there are two aspects to be taken into account: the individual's relations with his fellow workers in the factory, and his relations with his trade union. As to the former, it follows from what I have already said that I regard the individual's relations with his own working group as the most significant aspect. I dealt with this under the heading of organization, and said that one of the most important problems in modern industrial organization is to discover what in each case is the effective working group as the primary unit on which to build up the whole organizational structure. I said that each group should be large enough to accomplish a complete operation, and small enough to give its individual members the sense of personal comradeship and the feeling that each has within his own group a significant part to play. I further explained my idea as to how these primary groups should fit into the whole organization. To that explanation I need add nothing further.

I turn now to the second aspect of the individual's association with his fellow workers—namely, his relations with his trade union. If a close fellowship is created between those who are working side by side within a factory, can this be fitted into the wider fellowship of the trade union? Or will there be a conflict of loyalties? I have already referred to the danger of such a conflict, and have expressed the view that it can and must be overcome. The national interest demands that the trade unions should give their support to firms which are striving to improve human relations and to weld all ranks into a genuine co-operating community. I noted, further, that this must involve a change in the traditional conception of the trade union's role. This is recognized now by most of the national trade union leaders; but that is not always the case with the district officials, and the full implementation of this change will necessarily take time. Moreover, if the trade unions are to fulfil their new role effectively, many of them will have to make changes in their own organization. They too have to face the problem of combining effective measures of decentralization with the central guidance required for a co-ordinated national policy. Much remains to be done to make the organization of the trade unions sufficiently sensitive to individual opinion and activity, without, on the one hand, becoming split by sectionalization or, on the other, failing to fulfil their national industrial responsibilities. If the unions can solve these problems of organization and at the same time adopt the role of constructive partnership in the effort to improve human relations and productivity, then it will be possible for each individual trade union member to combine the satisfactions of union comradeship and comradeship in the working group of his factory.

But it must be recognized that the perfect achievement of these objects will not be easy, and that much goodwill is required on all sides. My own hope is that the present national emergency can be an effective force to bring all together.

FIVE

THE VALUE OF RESEARCH ON HUMAN FACTORS AND HUMAN RELATIONS IN INDUSTRY

I WANT now to give brief consideration to a subject which has a bearing on all the questions which I have discussed. I have throughout urged that mere goodwill is not enough, and that there is a need for first-class intellectual effort both in working out the best practical arrangements in matters of human relations and also in studying the nature of the problems, and I have specifically mentioned certain current research projects. I believe that a scientific approach to the study of human factors in industry can be of great value and that it is a moral duty for those who (on 'both sides') are concerned with the practical conduct of industry to stimulate and support this kind of approach. There is, however, considerable misunderstanding and confusion about what is the proper scope for scientific research in this matter. On the one hand, exaggerated claims are made (to which I shall refer in a later section), while, on the other hand, there is a good deal of suspicion and scepticism about the conception of a scientific study of human factors. In order to get a correct appreciation of what can usefully be done, it is helpful to review the kind of problems which need study. In earlier parts of this lecture I have touched on a number of these. As I see it, they can really be classified into five main groups:

Industrial Health (physical and mental)
'Human Engineering' (fitting the job to the man)

Selection and Training (fitting the man to the job)
Work Measurement (assessing the job)
Human Relations and Human Behaviour

Looking over this list, I think all must agree that the first four groups include subjects which are suitable for scientific study and on which more accurate knowledge is required. It is when one comes to the last group that one comes to difficulties and to the danger of mistaken ideas about what can be done. It is one thing to study the way in which different designs of working equipment affect the receptor and effector impulses of the human body. It is a totally different thing to examine questions of human behaviour—such questions as why a particular group of men dislike their foreman, or what have been the under-lying causes of trouble among the London dock workers or of any of the recent 'unofficial' strikes. And here, before I state my ideas about what can usefully be done, I want most strongly to emphasize once more certain things that I have already said. In considering human behaviour, one must always take into account that each individual is a unique personality. When in an earlier passage I quoted G. K. Chesterton's description of St. Francis of Assisi, I endorsed the implied warning against research workers who may look on men merely as units to be added to the spoils of some social policy or to provide data for hypotheses and conclusions in a research report. Each individual remains unique and incalculable, to be treated with sympathy and understanding as a personality, never as a mere unit. But, having said this, I can go on to express a belief that there is an immense amount of valuable work to be done in applying scientific method to the study of all the influences which affect the individual. There is an urgent need to find methods of precision to replace the subjective opinions and assumptions on which far too many judgements and policies are now in ordinary practice based. Let me give some illustrations of the kind of studies which I have in mind:

First I would put the need for extensive observational studies of contemporary conditions, either within industry or outside it, which can be expected to have a broad influence on the position. I have already mentioned a number of these. Thus, within industry there are such matters as the working of joint consultative methods; the methods for the selection and training of foremen; different methods for calculating the weekly wage packet; labour turnover, with its causes and effects; trade union organization and the influence of different types of organization on human relations within different industries. Or, to turn to influences outside industry, there are, for example, the effects of compulsory National Service on the young industrial entrant; the effects of school education on attitudes to work; the conditions affecting the transition from school to work; the effects of social security provisions; the effects of different kinds of living conditions and social environment. Then, again, there is much to be done in the way of historical studies: systematic studies of the history of different industries which might throw light on why certain industries (e.g. iron and steel) or certain companies have been abnormally free from strikes, and why others have had a very heavy strike incidence. Again, there is much value to be gained from intensive studies of particular situations—for example, the kind of study to which I have referred as one of the projects sponsored by the Human Factors Panel, which has been carried out by the Tavistock Institute in an engineering firm which is trying to work out an advanced system of 'industrial democracy'. Next there is a different kind of work which I have at many points advocated—namely, the continuous objective observation of day-to-day happenings in industry to be carried out by firms which are trying out new methods of production or new forms of organizations. And, finally, there is a need for profound studies of situations where acute trouble has arisen—for example, the recent trouble in the London Docks.

By systematic studies of this kind, it should be possible to build up a valuable body of knowledge as to the way in which various influences can affect human behaviour and human relations in industry. It ought to be possible to evolve a system which will enable those who hold responsible positions (whether in the ranks of government or of industrial managements or of the trade unions) to maintain a sensitive appreciation of the way in which people are reacting to current measures and conditions. Not only industrial leaders, but also the Government—above all, a Socialist Government—should be constantly on the alert to watch the indirect social reactions of their conduct and their policies.

In all these ways scientific method and knowledge can be a valuable aid to those who carry responsibilities the exercise of which affects the lives of their fellow men. My theme has been that to make the fullest use of this aid is a moral duty for all who carry such responsibilities; that this is, in fact, a duty included in those which are enjoined by Christ's two commandments.

SIX

SUMMARY OF ARGUMENT UP TO THIS POINT

I MUST NOW sum up what I have been trying to say.

I have considered human relations in industry as having three aspects: first, the relations of 'management' with 'workers', considered in terms of the responsibilities of the former; second, the relations of the workers with management, considered in terms of the workers' response; and, third, the relations of the workers with each other, including relations with the trade unions While making this distinction, I emphasized that the three aspects are in practice interdependent and inseparable.

On the first aspect, my thesis has been that, taking Christ's second commandment as stating the guiding principle, the primary responsibility of 'management' is to do everything possible to ensure for the workers that their industrial work fits in with, and forms part of, a good life in the highest sense. I have said that this means that at the very lowest, industrial work should be so handled that it can be regarded as a dignified activity, a necessity of nature, a condition of self-respect, not a positive evil imposed unnecessarily by the selfishness or incompetence of employers and capitalists. But I have added that management must not be satisfied with this 'very lowest' conception. They should strive in every way both to increase the opportunities for creative satisfaction in the work in itself and also to ensure that it fits in harmoniously with a satisfactory social setting for the workers' lives outside the factory.

To achieve these objects, no mere impulse of goodwill is enough. The love enjoined on every man by Christ's two commandments—both love of God and love of his neighbours—must be exercised, not only with all his heart and soul and strength, but with all his mind. In terms of responsibilities of management, this means first that management must make itself functionally efficient, and this must be seen as a moral duty. It means, secondly, that intense intellectual effort must be directed to evolving the best possible arrangements on a number of matters affecting human relations—such as organization (clear arrangements for the definition and decentralization of responsibilities), working conditions and health (physical and mental), arrangements for fitting the job to the man and the man to the job, pay (which must be adequate and fair), methods of communication and joint consultation (as a means to create a co-operating community in which all have a chance to understand the purpose of their work and to influence the way in which it is handled). The intellectual effort should include scientific research on many questions.

I have recognized the problems created by the conditions of modern industry—the size of industrial concerns and the methods of mass production. But I have argued that they can be solved. The size of a large concern need not make its management impersonal and inhuman if the right form of decentralized organization is adopted. The disadvantage of mass production can be overcome if all possible steps are taken for fitting the job to the man and the man to the job, for good communications and joint consultation, and for creating harmonious working groups. In a sense, 'craftsmanship' can be transferred from the individual to the group.

It has been an implication of my argument that to work for objectives affecting the condition of the workers is a primary responsibility of management, and that the means to secure them must be a first charge on every industrial undertaking. It must be recognized, for example, that no true profit has been earned except *after* making provision for all that is required to provide adequate pay and satisfactory working conditions for the workers. It follows from my statement of this as a primary responsibility of management that I regard this duty in regard to the workers as ranking, according to a Christian scale of values, higher than duties concerned with the external results of industrial activity. I do not underrate the absolute importance of those duties, but, relatively to the duty of satisfying what I have described at the 'first charge', I consider that they have in current discussion hitherto received more than their proper share of attention.

Turning to the 'second aspect'—the workers' response —the efforts of management cannot succeed unless this is adequate. All ranks in industry must recognize that the undertaking of creative work in a spirit of service is an essential condition for a good life on this earth. The provision of the material conditions for such a life can only be made secure, or worth securing, if all members recognize their responsibilities to the community.

Finally, as to the third aspect—the relations of the workers with each other—what chiefly matters is to build up effective working groups within each factory. Such groups must be part of a wider fellowship of two kinds: of the factory and of the trade union. The unions have an important part to play. They should give their support to those firms which are trying to build up a genuine co-operating community within the factory (not holding back because of a fear of conflict of loyalties), and this must be seen as part of a change in the whole conception of their role, a change from the conception of merely fighting for the interests of one side in industry against the other to the conception of a co-operative effort with management to improve the processes of production.

While I have fully recognized that there are many difficult problems to be solved, that progress must be slow, and that patience and courage are necessary, I have expressed the final conclusion that, if 'management' in general throughout British industry now plays its part efficiently and in the right spirit, then there is reason to hope for a response on the workers' side sufficient to keep the way open for continuing progress. The stipulation that management's part must be played in 'the right spirit' means that it must seek to create good human conditions and establish the right human relations as ends in themselves and not *merely* as a means for getting better production results.

And about this I have one more observation. At many points (for example, in dealing with joint consultation or the maintenance of full employment), I have recognized the difficulties that must be expected by those who take what I have called the progressive view. They may meet many disappointments, and even failure. But my central thought has been that today we have got to make a choice which cannot be evaded and which—put crudely, but, I believe, truly—depends on our answer to the question: Do we believe in playing down to the worst elements in human nature or in playing up to the best?

To this question the Christian can only give one answer. Here is a point at which we can see one of the essential meanings of Christian love. St. Paul, in his First Epistle to the Corinthians, has given us the words.

SEVEN

THE EFFECTS OF THE GENERAL ECONOMIC SYSTEM

IS A COMPLETE CHANGE OF THE ECONOMIC SYSTEM NECESSARY?

I MUST NOW turn back to a question of which I took note in my preliminary remarks (p. 21). Have I in all that I have said been evading the real issue? Is it possible to have anything like the right human relations in industry without a complete change of the present economic system? Ought Christians to concentrate on working for this?

I have deliberately left these questions to the end because I wanted to concentrate attention on the objects to be achieved and to consider them in terms of practical measures. To start with an argument about systems seems to me to involve the risk of a confusion between means and ends. I certainly do not want to get involved as a partisan in the present political controversy about State *versus* private ownership in industry. Indeed, that particular controversy does not really affect my main theme. We have got to face the fact that in this country (and this is true of the whole human race, except in a few still undeveloped parts of the world) we have brought ourselves into a position in which we cannot earn our daily bread except on the basis of factory production in which large numbers have to work together in organized fashion, using equipment which they cannot themselves supply, working for pay, subject to some measure of discipline and leadership and some form of central direction and

G

guidance. This is a condition which creates problems in the relationships of men with each other and men with their work which cannot be evaded. Certainly the transfer of industry to State ownership will not eliminate them. All the problems which I have discussed must arise, and all the measures which I have advocated will be required, whether the industries are owned by the State or by private citizens. And it is these things—the things which determine whether daily breadwinning work in industry can provide the foundation for a good human life—which really matter when one is considering the application of Christian principles to human relations in industry. I might then, so far as my main purpose is concerned, have left the matter at that. Since, however, there are many people who believe in the transfer to State ownership as a matter of principle, and since I think that hopes based on such a transfer alone will be disappointed, I must express my views on the matter.

At the outset, I must make it quite clear that I do not want to argue against the general idea of nationalization as a matter of principle. I personally agree, for example, that the nationalization of the coal-mines was an inevitable step and that the position today in that particular industry would have been far worse if it had not been taken. Further, I am not one of those who think that a great principle of essential liberties is at stake. I regard it rather as an issue of expediency, to be settled according to circumstances for each industry—the essential question being what methods in each case will best serve the national interest. If I question the idea of universal nationalization, it is as a matter affecting the efficient working of industry. As to that, I think that our great problem today is to avoid a top-heavy, rigid, over-centralized organization and to preserve flexibility and scope for individual initiative, and, taking into account the great complexity of the main part of British industry,

I can see no better practical method of decentralization than to allow industrial units to be operated by people who have their own money at stake and stand to fall or prosper by their own efforts. If, however, the continuance of private enterprise is to be defended on these grounds, there are two essential conditions to be fulfilled. First, some system of regulation must be devised to ensure that private industries are operated in the public interest. Secondly, the industries must fulfil the condition with which I have been concerned throughout this lecture and which I do regard as a matter of principle—namely, the condition of affording a basis for a good life for those working in them.

The real questions, therefore, are: whether privately owned industries can satisfy those two conditions, or whether, because they cannot, a change to State ownership is necessary.

As to the first condition, I do not wish to be dogmatic; but my own belief is that it should not be impossible to devise the right form of regulation. I recognize that it requires a considerable advance in attitudes and technique on the part of both the Government and the leaders of industry. The latter in particular have got to recognize that private enterprise cannot claim or hope to survive unless it can establish that it is working in the public interest, and that they themselves must collaborate with the Government to fulfil national policies. For this purpose, they must be ready to study the national economic position and maintain a rigid scrutiny of the results of their own operations. Industries must organize themselves for this purpose rather than for protecting their own sectional interests. There is vast room for improvement here. But, having watched the great changes in outlook which, in recent times, have taken place under the stress of national emergency, I feel it justifiable to hope that a satisfactory system of regulation can be evolved.

As to the second question, what has to be considered is whether the handling of human relations on lines which I have advocated is likely to be done better in nationalized than in privately owned industries. Again I do not wish to be dogmatic. It would be unfair to pronounce judgement today on the recently nationalized industries, such as coal and transport, since they have had vast initial difficulties to contend with. But one cannot entirely ignore experience to date, while there is much longer experience available in certain cases, for example, the Royal Ordnance Factories. Moreover, in making comparisons, it is not only the negative evidence of shortcomings in the nationalized industries which is to be taken into account: there is also the positive evidence of what has been done in privately owned concerns. On all the evidence that I have seen, it is justifiable to say that, in the movement toward what I have described as right methods for handling human relations, there have been greater advances in privately owned concerns than in the nationalized industries. It is in private concerns that one can find the most hopeful experiments in the development of such methods as joint consultation, and in the building up of groups working for a common purpose. Further, I have in an earlier passage—for example, that dealing with pay—given my reasons for concluding that the mere elimination of private shareholders does not seem to have overcome the intrinsic difficulties.

As I have said, I do not wish to make too much of all this in these early days as a charge against the nationalized industries; but it is legitimate to regard it as evidence against the argument that things must inevitably be bad in private enterprise concerns, and that it is intrinsically impossible in their case to move toward right human relations. On the contrary, I believe that privately owned industry can work in fulfilment of the principle that industrial employment should afford the basis for a good life; and on that belief my conclusion is that what Christians should strive for is to strengthen the influences which can exert pressure to secure observance of this principle.

And for the strengthening of these influences there is very great need. I certainly do not want to paint too rosy a picture of what is actually happening in industry today. There are some bright spots which give a foundation for hope; but, throughout large sections, the general standard in practices and attitudes falls far short of what I have advocated. The need is to establish right standards of individual and corporate behaviour and to work for these by insisting on publication of more and fuller information of the results of every enterprise, and by educating the public to use their power either as wage-earners or consumers to resist abuses. There is a need, too, for the Government to develop better methods of regulation and guidance, and for private industry, as I have already said, to organize itself for collaborating with the Government and for studying the impact of its activities on national economic conditions. The trade unions too can do a great deal—in fact, they can be the most powerful influence of all. One particular line for action I have mentioned in an earlier passage: the trade unions should bring pressure to bear on the inefficient firms who say they 'can't afford' to maintain right conditions. It must be accepted as a principle that what is required to maintain adequate conditions for the workers is a first charge on income, and that profits are not truly earned until that first charge has been met. The trade unions can do even more by working as constructive partners with management for the improvement of productive efficiency and by supporting the efforts of those firms that are trying to create the right kind of industrial relations and to build up a true co-operative community within each factory. Finally, everybody who in any way can influence public opinion can help. I believe that the Churches can play a great part here, but I would venture to urge that what the Churches should do is to stand for principles—the principles of right human relations in industry—rather than to advocate particular forms of system and thus get involved in technical controversies.

In all these ways, good influences can be strengthened, and my own belief is that, if economic enterprise is run mainly as an activity independent of the State, it may actually be easier to maintain effective pressure for right action and effective sanctions against abuse than if it is all included in a totalitarian State organization.

I must add two general reflections.

In present conditions it is a change of outlook, a change in our scale of values, which is required much more than a change in external forms. As Victor Gollancz has said:[1]

A technically socialist State in the economic sense can be as illiberal, as materialistic, as inhuman as a capitalist one; indeed, it can be more so.

And he has charged the present Government with being still wholly capitalist in its choice of incentives and of being in its general tone materialistic. Every form of human system will be liable to abuse as long as men seek selfish ends, and I believe that the 'power motive' or the 'publicity motive' may be even more dangerous than the 'profit motive'—certainly more than the profit motive as now limited and controlled.

Finally, in expressing these views, I am influenced by the belief that for Christians interested in practical affairs the essential question is: What are the best next steps which are practicable? We can only move from where we are, and we have no magic power to jump to final perfection, although in choosing next steps we must keep our vision of

[1] *Our Threatened Values*, p. 19.

that final perfection before us. In this matter of our national economic system we must surely accept the fact that there is no chance, in the visible future, of this country adopting a complete system of national ownership of all the means of production and distribution. For any period which we can foresee, a large section of economic enterprise is bound to continue under private ownership and direction. Surely, then, the right course is to devise and operate every possible measure for making that system work as nearly as possible in harmony with Christian principles. To take the line that nothing short of a revolutionary change of system can be of any avail seems to me to be an unhelpful approach to the problems which we have to face today, and one which is liable to concentrate people's attention on means rather than on ends.

SOME FURTHER REFLECTIONS ON THE ECONOMIC SYSTEM

In the preceding paragraphs I have considered the significance of our present economic system by giving my views on one particular form of possible change. I have made clear that I do not hold these views dogmatically, and my main point has been that a mere change from private to State ownership of industry is not of fundamental importance, since it will not by itself alter or solve our essential problems. I believe, in fact, that to understand the present situation and what is required to effect a true improvement, it is necessary to search much deeper both into our fundamental economic condition, and also into the influences which affect human conduct.

For this purpose, it is valuable to look back into history, since the historical background gives a sense of perspective and proportion, and one can better understand the present position if one follows out the developments which have led up to it. When I look back in this way, I find myself confirmed in the conclusion that those who attach great weight to outward forms of human organization may thereby encourage undue hopes of what can be achieved by any mere change of system. I think Reinhold Niebuhr expresses an essential truth when he says that if man 'attributes the admitted evils of human history to specific social and historical causes he involves himself in begging the question; for all these specific historical causes of evil are revealed, upon close analysis, to be no more than particular consequences and historical configurations of evil tendencies in man himself'.[2]

Human history, as I see it, can be interpreted as a series of dramas with a recurrent theme: Act I—men's selfish struggle for worldly objectives (power or wealth); Act II—the corruption and abuses produced by success in attaining these objectives; Act III—reaction or revolt against the abuses leading to a revolutionary or reforming change of system, political, social, economic. And then the whole cycle begins again with its three phases, possibly different in form, but with essentially the same significance and sequence. Martin Luther put what is really the same conception in a different way when he likened humanity to the drunken peasant who falls off his horse on one side and then, if he is put back from that, falls off on the other. One kind of abuse may be corrected by a change to a new system, but that will merely give openings for new forms of abuse—unless human nature itself changes. There can be no abuse-proof system made and operated by man. I agree with the warning given by Victor Gollancz in the passage which I have quoted, and with the fears of Nicolas Berdyaev that socialism, as he saw it coming, must lead to the socialization of conscience and soul and the supremacy of materialistic values.

All this may be very obvious, but I think it needs saying. Having said it, however, I must go on to recognize that

[2] *Nature and Destiny of Man*, Vol. I, p. 2.

the form of the economic system is an important matter. Different systems may have differing effects in the strength of the stimulus given to human weaknesses and in the type of weakness which is especially encouraged. And, of course, human beings (unless they are hopeless pessimists, which I am not) must hope that each stage of 'correction' will produce a system which has less temptation and better safeguards against abuse, so that, in spite of the sequence of ebb and flow, there may be a slowly advancing tide of human progress. For these reasons it is important to understand the exact nature and historical origins of the 'system' under the influence of which the present state of our social and economic life has developed. As an aid to this kind of understanding, some of the most valuable contributions have been made by the scholars and theologians who have looked at historical developments from the Christian point of view. I have particularly in mind two series of Scott Holland Lectures: Professor Tawney's on *Religion and the Rise of Capitalism* and Canon Demant's, just completed, on *Religion and the Decline of Capitalism*. I wish I had time to comment on these more fully. I must content myself with a few reflections on Canon Demant's lectures, which I have found of fascinating interest.

At the outset, it is necessary to say something about terminology. The word 'capitalism' is often used in a way which tends to create misunderstanding about the true nature of our present problems. The essence of a 'capitalistic' system is that economic activities under it require the building up of capital resources (buildings, machinery, working capital), and that this can only be done if people accumulate capital by forbearing to consume all the proceeds of current production.[3] Now, of course, some-

[3] Whether capital expenditure is delayed until 'savings' have actually been accumulated, or is undertaken on the basis of anticipating savings through the use of all the ingenious credit devices which men have developed, does not affect the essential nature of the process.

thing of this kind has gone on since the dawn of history. The primitive agriculturist who keeps back some seed for the next sowing instead of eating it all is, as Canon Demant has pointed out, a 'capitalist' in this sense. But— and this is the point I want to make—the element of 'capital' acquired an entirely new significance in the methods of production developed after the Industrial Revolution, and this importance of the capital element was a major distinctive characteristic of the nineteenth-century economic system. Its practical implications are two-fold: first, there must be arrangements which induce individuals, or force the community, to make such savings from current consumption as are required to provide, maintain, and develop the necessary capital equipment; and, secondly, a state of affairs is created in which the bulk of the population can only earn their daily bread on a foundation of capital resources and equipment which they cannot themselves provide. Now, of 'capitalism' in this sense (which I maintain is the only accurate sense in which to use the word) there certainly is no sign of a decline today. In this sense, Russia is the leading capitalist country, since the Russian series of five-year plans represents the most determined effort in human history to cut down current consumption for the sake of building up capital resources. In the rest of the world, too, the relative importance of machinery—or capital equipment—is markedly increasing. So far as changes are taking place in this country, the truth is that these represent, not a decline of capitalism, but a move from a system of free, privately owned capitalistic enterprise to a system where such enterprise is either owned by the State or subject to extensive State regulation.

I think it important to recognize this distinction, and I think it unfortunate that Canon Demant has had to use such an expression as 'decline of capitalism' in the title of his lectures. I cannot blame him for this, since he is using the word 'capitalism' in one of the senses in which it had been used ever since Karl Marx wrote. Moreover, he himself has most lucidly explained what he means by the term. He says that he is talking of 'capitalism', not in the sense that I have just stated—a sense in which 'all civilization is capitalist'—but of 'the thing which is generally known as capitalism—a much newer and short-lived event —namely, the phase in which social and economic relations became determined almost entirely by the free play of the buying and selling, or the market interaction.' And in another passage he quotes Max Weber's appreciation of the modern as compared with the medieval system:

Hence the difference does not lie in the degree of any impulse to make money; but in the removal of an ethic based on religion which places certain psychological sanctions (not of an economic character) on the maintenance of an attitude prescribed by it, sanctions which mere worldly wisdom does not place at its disposal.

He then states as a central question for his examination:

What could possibly have brought about such a radical, unique and extraordinary change in human behaviour as that represented by the emergency of economic life as an autonomous activity?

'Capitalism' therefore for Canon Demant connotes these two characteristics: the dominance of economic life as a law unto itself, and the regulation of economic life by the market principle. And capitalism in this sense he sees as suffering a decline or a 'great reversal' by 'the bending of economic processes to social ends', a decline which

is to be regarded not as the beginning of a new era in history but as the end of a short-lived experiment.

Now, this appreciation I regard as illuminating and in a sense true; but it is not the whole truth, and may, I think, suggest ideas which are misleading, particularly if one is trying, as I am in this lecture, to find answers to the questions as to what our conduct ought to be in present conditions and by what practicable steps we can, from where we now stand, move in the direction of true progress. If one is trying to answer such questions, it is misleading to regard the capitalism of the nineteenth century as a 'short-lived phase' from which we can return to earlier conditions. The nineteenth-century system had other essential features which cannot be obliterated. There is the feature of the increased importance of the 'capital' element which I have already noted. And beyond this there is the fact that, as a result of nineteenth-century capitalism, the economic processes of life have attained a much greater significance in the total life of society than they ever had in any previous stage in human history. We in this small island, by developing a manufacturing industry working with vast capital equipment combined with a system of international trade supported by every kind of ingenious financial device, have enabled a population of fifty millions to grow up and acquire its daily bread.[4] And thereby we have given ourselves an economic task differing absolutely in kind from that which we had with a population of some ten millions, as it was at the beginning of the nineteenth century, and have saddled ourselves with new burdens and problems from which there can be no escape. If therefore the nineteenth-century system is to be changed, it is essential to understand exactly what were its methods and principles, in what way they were wrong, and how we can modify them without ignoring the realities which past history has created for us.

I will attempt very briefly to summarize my own appreciation of the 'nineteenth-century system'.

First, as a general observation, I do not think it is

[4] It is worth remembering that in this country only 5 per cent of the working population are engaged in agriculture (i.e. producing our daily bread), whereas even in the industrialized United States the figure is over 17 per cent, and in France 33 per cent.

exactly correct to say, as Canon Demant implies, that the nineteenth-century ideas involved giving economic aims supremacy over moral aims. Rather they regarded all true progress as dependent on economic progress and, in a sense, they identified the two. It is this identification which is wrong. If we condemn the nineteenth century for wrongly identifying the two, are we quite certain that this identification is not still being made today? I certainly can feel no such certainty.

Passing to the particular tenets of the nineteenth-century creed, I should put them shortly in this way:

(i) Economic progress is the surest way to provide true human progress.

(ii) Economic progress will best be stimulated (a) by giving the incentive of personal gain free play, (b) by free competition, making for the survival of the fittest and the elimination of the inefficient, and (c) by the free-market system, which is essential partly as the only sure way of fixing a 'just price' for goods and services, and partly as a means for ensuring that productive activity is directed into the right channels, thereby avoiding unhealthy results like over-production of certain things.

That was the theory. Its practice tended to create the idea that all values were commensurable in terms of money, and that the degree of profitability was a correct guide to the choice between different activities. This theory and practice were supported (to quote Canon Demant) 'by the doctrine of the hidden hand which behind the scenes of human will and intelligence made all things work together for good whether men loved God or not' or, as J. M. Keynes used to put it, 'the astonishing belief that the nastiest motives of the nastiest men somehow or other work for the best results in the best of all possible worlds'.

And that itself is only a paraphrase of Archbishop Whately's statement (quoted by Canon Demant): 'It is curious to observe how, through a wise and beneficent arrangement of Providence, men thus do the greatest service to the public when they are thinking of nothing but their own gain.'

What has happened to all that doctrine now? We have learned by hard experience that it was as vain and groundless as other forms of Victorian optimism. The theory has failed. Its standard of values was wrong. It has failed, even judged by its own standards. Free competition, for example, has shown that it could become so-called 'uneconomic' competition, and the practitioners of the theory have themselves sought defences against it, either by their own concerted arrangements or by asking for government 'protection'. It has failed because it has led to results which the social conscience of the country cannot tolerate—for example, the mass unemployment of the inter-war years. It can be argued that the failure in results has been essentially due to two world wars, which caused dislocations of a totally unnatural and abnormal kind. But that line of argument does no more than point to one essential cause of its failure—namely, that men cannot be relied on to behave in the way that the Victorian economic theory presupposed: that is to say, by always choosing the course which is likely to 'pay' best. (Thus Norman Angel proved in *The Great Illusion* that war could not 'pay' at the very moment when the era of world wars was beginning.) The practical fact remains that the theory cannot be relied on to work in the way that the Victorians assumed it would work, and, what is still more important, that it led to the creation of a wrong scale of values.

In recognizing this failure, however, it is very important not to misinterpret its practical implications. We cannot free ourselves from the result of the conditions which the past has created for us, and even if we condemn the Victorian theory it does not necessarily follow that we can immediately abandon all its practices. Let me take the ideas of competition as a test of efficiency, and of a free market as a means to settle a 'just price' for products. In the actual conditions which have been built up there is a value in these ideas to which no one can be blind who has studied the working of synthetic price-fixing methods, such as had to be adopted during the war in contracts for production of war weapons, or as are continuing under some of the peace-time price controls. These methods all inevitably tend to make it too easy for the inefficient to make profits and have other bad effects. But there is another and much more vitally important consideration to be taken into account. We in this country depend on international trade for our daily bread, and as long as this is so we cannot disregard the need for competitive efficiency nor escape altogether from the market system. We with our preponderant dependence on external trade cannot abolish the market system and competition in our domestic economy without grave peril to our ability to keep our place in external markets.

I can turn from that to other features of less vital significance. Take, for example, the use of money as a general measure of value. The complex working of modern business can hardly be carried on without that. Also, in a sense, the money criterion has value as a test of realism. When John Bright, walking home one day, found a group of neighbours standing round the poor old carrier whose horse, his only source of livelihood, had fallen down and broken its knees and smashed the cart, he said to those who were loud in their words of sorrow and sympathy: 'Well, friends, I'm sorry five pounds. How much are you sorry?' And he then and there started a collection which set the old man up again. That perhaps is a trivial illustration; but it has a suggestive significance.

I have been trying to indicate the sort of things which have to be taken into account before one talks loosely about getting away from the practices of the old system. There are many more. And the crucial question to which they all point is this: How far and in what ways is it practicable to proceed in what Canon Demant calls 'bending economic processes to social ends *extra commercium*'.

I entirely agree that this indicates a right aim; but I see the possibility of dangerously wrong interpretations of the words 'bending economic processes'. We have indeed got to recognize that economic processes and economic results are no more than means to an end, and also that, in pursuing economic purposes, we must not break moral laws. But the economic sphere is a distinct sphere, and it has its own true laws which cannot be broken. Its own true laws are not those of the Victorian ideas, which rested on the erroneous assumption that human beings will always behave in a certain way under the influence of economic motives. The true laws are the very simple laws that a nation as a whole cannot go on consuming more than it produces, and that the national economic enterprise must be run at profit in the sense that it must produce a balance over and above its operating expenses (i) to pay for the cost of government and of a great number of directly unproductive services, and (ii) to provide a margin which will ensure the maintenance and expansion of its capital equipment and a sufficient inducement in the form of return on capital to influence people to save that margin from current consumption. It may be that the national interest demands that a particular industry shall be carried on even though it cannot itself produce profits; but such a position can only be supported out of the profits of other industries—which must therefore be increased. The total national economic enterprise cannot be run at a loss without national ruin. The 'profit' motive, about which so much has been written, may have for social reasons to be regulated and controlled, but the profit criterion cannot be ignored; and there is real danger that in preaching the supremacy of social purposes this may happen. (There is, incidentally, another danger very present today: that the 'social purposes' themselves may be wrong and be interpreted entirely in terms of material objectives; but that raises other issues.)

The observations which I have made are intended as suggestive reflections rather than exhaustive treatment. They lead me to the following conclusions: The right course is to study at what points the working of our system has produced evil results, and to concentrate attention on devising forms of regulation for correcting those results, and effective sanctions against abuses. Very briefly, the outstanding evils have been, first, gross inequalities of of wealth, secondly, a wrong scale of values expressed in the supremacy of money in all spheres, and, thirdly, a wrong invocation of economic laws as justifying conditions of work incompatible with a dignified human life.

I regard recent experience as showing that much can be done to reduce inequalities of wealth without destroying the working of the present economic machine. I believe, further, that the policy and conditions which have been forced on us during the last years have tended to diminish the dominance of the money-making motive and to put money more nearly into its proper place in our scale of values. I welcome both these developments, and consider that they can, and should, go much farther. Under both headings, however, there are many dangers to be avoided, and there is need to watch carefully the reactions of our policies and to study the best means of achieving our national objectives. To discuss adequately all that is involved in this would require another lecture.

For the purpose of my subject, it is the third kind of evil which matters most and on which I have concentrated my attention.

As to this, my central question has been whether it is possible to conduct industry in our present economic system in a way which is sufficiently profitable to maintain our national existence and at the same time to make industrial work something which fits in with a 'good life' for those who are engaged in it. I believe profoundly that a way forward toward this objective can be found, and that the best hope of finding that way is to seek guidance from Christian principles. I have tried to show what this means in terms of practical measures. It is on developing the best form for such measures that all available energy, intellectual ability, and goodwill should be concentrated.

To promote a great new drive in this direction, two things are needed: first, a revival of Christian faith; secondly, the strengthening of a practical conviction that men *can* find a way to give expression to Christian principles in the daily round even as it exists today.

EIGHT

SOME DANGERS AND OPPORTUNITIES OF THE PRESENT TIMES

BEFORE I close, I want to glance back over some features in the contemporary scene which are relevant to my subject and which seem to me to have special significance as indicating crucial dangers and opportunities.

The Danger that Religion may be exploited as a Means to Material Ends

First, there is our desperate need to improve the national productive output. This in itself creates a great opportunity. At no time since the Industrial Revolution has it been so clear that improvement is required in the interests of the workers themselves. Our national survival depends upon it, and it offers the only chance for improving the workers' standards of living. All can see that there is no longer any appreciable margin for increasing the workers' share of the national product by reducing the share of others. It is clear, too, that there is no reserve of unemployed labour. The only hope, therefore, lies in making more effective the efforts of those who are already at work. The urgency of the need and the clear common interest of all sections of the community in meeting it make the present a unique occasion for evoking a new kind of co-operative effort. This is one of the great opportunities of our times. But it is balanced by two dangers: the danger that concentration on material objectives will distract attention from higher values, and the danger that right action will be sought not for its own sake, but merely as a temporary expedient to overcome immediate material difficulties.

I have already commented on the latter danger in the field of industrial relations. What I want to emphasize now is that the danger in this field is an example of a general danger of the present times which extends much more widely. We must all of us be aware of individuals or groups who advocate a revival of Christianity 'as the only sure way to combat Communism'. At many points today there may be, as Sir Walter Moberly has said of certain university circles, a 'new-found interest in religion' which 'may resemble too much the attitude of Gibbon's magistrate, the Christian religion being welcomed as a useful social cement, which is calculated to preserve continuity and to counteract unsettlement'.[1] Or to quote Sir Walter Moberly again:

Religious sentiment may be fostered as a means to an end for the purposes of 'moral rearmament', as a bulwark of the institutions of the country and as a counterweight to Communism or to other revolutionary forces. For such purposes emotional awareness of a purpose at once transcending and governing the life of the individual and the whole contemporary and terrestrial scene may be cultivated, while all theological doctrine is left in a convenient haze. But such exploitations of the Christian religion for ends other than its own would be the ultimate profanity.[2]

These are hard words, and I should not wish to pronounce this kind of judgement without qualification on all who are influenced by the contemporary movements to which they apply. It is difficult to keep a right balance in this matter. If the parlous condition of the world today, showing as it does into what depths of evil human beings can sink if they seek power or other world ends without regard for any higher law, is making men realize the need to seek guidance in religious faith, that, in itself is something which must be welcomed. Move-

[1] *The Crisis in the University*, p. 275.   [2] ibid., pp. 103-4.

ments based on such reaction can be turned to good. The crucial question is in what direction, once they are started, they are turned. Here surely is an opportunity for the Christian Churches. It is not enough merely to condemn or stand aloof from these movements. They mean something. They should be studied and understood. They show that all over the world today men are groping for some kind of faith and guidance. The Christian Churches should help people to understand how such movements may be guided on right courses, and how to avoid dangerous confusions of means with ends.

The Danger of Wrong Interpretations of what Science can do

A second kind of contemporary danger is that arising from a misconception of the contribution which the so-called 'social sciences' can make to the right handling of human situations and human problems.[3] An idea which runs through much of the contemporary 'social science' literature (and which has been propounded most clearly in books by the late Professor Elton Mayo, such as *The Social Problems of an Industrial Society*) is that the main cause of humanity's troubles today is the fact that men's 'social skills' have not advanced equally with their scientific and technical skills. It is the emphasis on the word 'skill' which alarms me. This is not merely a matter of skill. If, for example, we are to create the right human relations in industry, we need right moral attitudes more fundamentally than intellectual skill. Before studying psychology, we need to study *and accept* the principles of the New Testament. And for these principles there is no question of any need for 'advance'. They express eternal

[3] A good example of exaggerated claims made for the possible contribution of social science is to be found in a recently published American book, *The Proper Study of Mankind*, by Stuart Chase. On its wrapper is printed a recommendation from Julian Huxley, who says that the book 'makes us realize that Social Science is *the only way* in which man can hope to proceed from the conquest of nature to the rational control of himself'. (The italics are mine.)

truths which cannot change. We do, indeed, as I have at all points insisted, need skill (based on hard intellectual effort and scientific study) in working out methods for the application of these principles among all the complexities which we have created for ourselves in modern industrial society; but, unless the exercise of such skill is guided by the spirit of Christianity, unless our aims are regulated according to a true scale of values, the skill will not merely be as useless as a 'sounding brass or a tinkling cymbal', but can become an instrument of devastating evil. Dostoevski's Grand Inquisitor in *The Brothers Karamazov* shows what this can mean. Hitler and Stalin have given examples of consummate skill in the manipulation of mass psychology.

Science, in fact, can provide instruments for the fulfilment of men's purposes; but whether these are instruments for good or evil depends entirely on how the ultimate purposes are chosen, and for that choice science can give no guidance.

The error of which I am now speaking, and which, as I see it, runs through much of the current 'social science' literature, is in fact of a double nature.[4] First, there is the error of claiming for the concepts and generalizations of 'social science'—especially those concerning the behaviour of human personalities—a validity of the same nature as can be established in the field of the physical sciences; and, secondly, there is a misconception of what any kind of scientific knowledge can do. Both errors are important in relation to my subject; but in the present context it is with the danger of the second and wider error that I am

---

[4] I am very conscious that these references to current literature are superficial, and give inadequate recognition to the valuable work done by people like Elton Mayo or to the important function which can be performed by social science studies. I have, however, already at many points made clear my appreciation of that function and my ideas as to how it should be exercised (see especially pp. 89–92). It is against a dangerous confusion between scientific knowledge and moral judgements that I am protesting in the present passage.

concerned. If man is to take the right course at the present crucial moment in the history of humanity, then it is essential not to be misled by false ideas about what science can do. Science cannot solve man's moral problems. Science cannot explain for him the meaning of his existence. No scientific discovery can give him a scale of values or rules to regulate the dictates of his conscience. The thirty-eighth chapter of Job asks questions which no Newton or Darwin or modern atom-splitter can answer: 'Where wast thou when I laid the foundations of the earth? . . . Who hath put wisdom in the inward parts? Or who hath given understanding to the heart?'

NINE

CONCLUDING THOUGHTS

WHERE WE STAND TODAY

AND these last questions point to the thoughts with which
I close this lecture. In my opening paragraphs I said
that the conditions of these times give to us who are alive
today a unique responsibility and opportunity. I want to
emphasize this again in my conclusion. We stand at a
crucial point in human history, and, because of this, all
our actions and all our practical arrangements, even in
trivial daily matters, can have tremendous importance if,
by providing examples or opportunities, they help to turn
men's thoughts and methods in right directions.

This is a time to cast our eyes back over history and
consider the road which has brought us to the point where
we now stand and the choice of roads which lie before us.
If we are to look back in this way, it is the history of
Western civilization which has the chief significance,
since—and this, too, is one of the distinctive characteristics
of these times—humanity has just reached a point where
this world of ours is becoming in an entirely new sense
'one world', and, in this closing up of contacts between
races, the influence of decisive importance is the impact
on all nations of the ideas and techniques of Western
civilization. What is to happen to Western ideas? What
uses are to be made of the power given to man by Western
science and technology? These are crucial questions.

Looking at the story as one of Western civilization, we
can see in present conditions the logical development of
the movement which began with the Renaissance—a
movement started under the lead of scientists, humanists,
and artists, and guided by ideas, like Francis Bacon's,

that knowledge is power and that man by the use of such power can work out his own salvation.

Today we can look round the world and realize to what a pass these ideas have brought the human race. Man, with his vastly increased power based on scientific knowledge and invention, stands confronted with the prospect, not of his salvation, but of self-destruction—the destruction of human civilization. Never in human history has it been clearer that worldly societies must come to disaster whenever men think they can plan their progress without respect for a higher law. Never has it been clearer that without religious faith there can be no sure foundation for that respect.

This appreciation has, of course, all the inaccuracies of an over-simplification. It ignores the nobility in the original form of the ideas which inspired the Renaissance. It ignores all the history of the intervening centuries—the varying ways in which the surviving power of religious tradition or the fresh influence of great religious leaders like John Wesley have hitherto tempered and restrained the logical development of what I have called the Baconian doctrine. Nevertheless, I believe that my appreciation expresses the essential truth about the present position of mankind and that what matters supremely today is that there should be a general understanding of this truth.

If that is the position, how are men reacting to it? As I see it, there are, broadly, three main groups or lines of thought.

First, there are those who say in effect: 'The Baconian idea was right. Its implementation has hitherto been hampered by respect for ethical laws based largely on religious myths and superstitions. We shall make use of power without these inhibitions, and by its use we shall control the masses for purposes which we decide, and in this way we shall bring our form of order into the world.' With the leaders who say this may be classed all those who are willing to be led by them.

Second, there are those who differ from the first group

in that they stand for personal liberty and the individual's right to regulate his own existence, but who retain essentially materialistic ideas about existence. Members of this group claim to be realists. For some of them this means pessimism and the adoption of gloomy philosophies, such as Existentialism. Others still cherish the idea that man, by the advance of knowledge in the fields of both the physical and the social sciences, can move along the path of human progress, though they cannot explain how their own creed can enable them to judge what true 'progress' is.

Third and last, there are the people who feel the need for a religious faith to give a meaning to their existence. These, I am convinced, are the vast majority of mankind today. This group covers a wide and varied range of thought. It includes, of course, those fortunate beings who are sure of their religious faith; but beyond these there are vast numbers who are unsure, who are groping for some support to which they can hold, some light which can give them guidance, and who, either consciously or unconsciously, apprehend that what they need is something more than what their own reason or the observations of science can give them.

European man [wrote Nicolas Berdyaev, even before the last world war] stands amid a frightening emptiness. He no longer knows where the keystone of his life may be found, beneath his feet he feels no depths of solidity.[1]

That is a thought which has been echoed and expressed in many forms all round the world. In this country of ours it has not led to pessimism in the same way as on the Continent. On the contrary, it has I believe created a new receptiveness to the teachings of Christianity.

THE GREAT OPPORTUNITY

Here is the great opportunity. People today—and especially the rising generation—are hungry for a message.

[1] *The End of Our Times*, p. 189.

How can it be sent out to them, to use my own earlier phrase, 'on "wavelengths" to which ordinary people with their modern forms of thought can "tune in" '? I venture to urge that this is a question which the Christian Churches should now keep in the forefront of their attention. The answer, of course, is not a mere matter of outward form, nor can it be found merely by intellectual thought. It is faith that is needed, and faith must be aroused by the fervour and inspiration of individual leaders. Yet I believe that intellectual thought is needed too, and that this intellectual thought must be in accord with scientific concepts. In saying this, and in speaking of 'ordinary people with their modern forms of thought', I have in mind the observation of Professor Ortega y Gasset that every age has its own system of vital ideas and that the vital system of today is based on physical science. There is truth in this, and it leads me to a conclusion which I would put in this way. Although the kind of message for which I am pleading cannot rely for its positive success on intellectual grounds, it must be intellectually convincing in the sense that it must be able to overcome the negative influences of intellectual resistances and defences. And here there is occasion for encouragement. The walls of intellectual resistance today are much more ready to fall than they were a generation ago or in Victorian times. Science, with its own greater knowledge, has become more humble. Yet, although some (and the greatest) scientific thinkers appreciate the limitations of science, there are a number who do not. There is plenty of evidence of this today. Apart from what I have already said about current 'social science' literature, one can see recent broadcast talks and discussions on such subjects as the nature of the Universe as illustrating, not only how wide is the public interest in the scientific approach, but also into what confusion scientists can get when they pass from the straight recording of astronomic observations to expound their notions as to how the new knowledge of the spatial universe affects ideas on the meaning of human existence, and to imply that observation of the stars can help men to measure and understand mind and morality or personality and love. There is a danger here which cannot be ignored, and it is for this reason that I venture to stress the need for giving thought to handling what I may call the intellectual approach—to working out methods and forms of expression which will help ordinary people to understand what are, and must be, the limitations of scientific knowledge, to realize what a confusion of thought it is to allow religious faith to become entangled with scientific theories about the physical universe, and to satisfy themselves that it is 'intellectually practicable to be religious'.

RELIGIOUS FAITH AND ETHICAL PRINCIPLES

These last paragraphs have taken me far beyond the limited subject of my lecture; but they have been inspired by the same idea. My object throughout has been to consider practical ways by which ordinary people can be helped to make the Christian faith an effective influence in their daily lives, and the idea which underlies all that I have said is that for this purpose a mere emotional appeal is not enough.

There are two essential requirements. First, and above all, there must be a surely founded religious faith, and it has been with that in mind that, in these last paragraphs, I have urged the importance of meeting the hunger of ordinary people with a Christian message which, with their modern forms of thought, they can understand and find convincing. Second, there must be ethical principles which are clearly understood and recognized as applicable in real life, and it is that requirement which has provided the main theme of my lecture. I have given my interpretation of the ethical principles of Christianity, and I have tried to indicate practical ways for applying them in one important sphere of modern life—the sphere of industrial production. I have wished to voice my own profound conviction that it *is* possible to combine the efficient conduct of industry with the fulfilment of these Christian principles, and that the first duty of all who are, in any capacity, concerned with the conduct of industry is to devote thought to devising practical methods for achieving this high purpose.

THE NEED FOR A SIMPLE OPTIMISTIC FAITH

And this gives me the note on which I wish to end. The great need today is for a spirit of fighting optimism. By that I do not mean the unfounded optimism of Victorian times, which rested on the belief that men had discovered the way of true human progress. I mean an optimism which sees the problems, but refuses to accept them as insoluble, an optimism which recognizes the threats and perils which surround us, but refuses to abandon the faith that human life has purpose and meaning and that there is an end worth striving for.

The world needs a renewal of a simple, optimistic faith. It is for our country above all others to show the way. But to do that we must not only live according to that faith, but also demonstrate that we can make a success of our own society. And, since ours is essentially an industrial society, a first condition of success is to achieve the purposes with which I have been concerned in this lecture: to establish good human relations in industry and to make industrial employment the foundation for worthy human lives.

For that we have today a unique opportunity. The perils and difficulties which surround us should be both a challenge and an inspiration. Never before in living memory has there been for all who have the chance to work so clearly a worthwhile job to do. And that, as I have urged, is the foundation of happiness in worldly life. But this opportunity will be missed and all these hopes will fail without the strength and guidance of religious faith.

INDEX